Also by Mick Wall

MARKET SQUARE HEROES: The Authorised Story of Marillion
DIARY OF A MADMAN: The Official Biography of Ozzy Osbourne

GUNS N' ROSES

GUNS N' ROSES

The Most Dangerous Band in the World

Mick Wall

New York

CONTENTS

AUTHOR'S ACKNOWLEDGEMENTS

This book could not have been written without the 24-hour-a-day assistance of the following people: most especially Linda La Ban, Richard Boote and Andy Amber Clark – their love was my drug. Thanks also to Geoff Barton for his continuing patience and goodwill, and Susan Hill and Helen Gummer of Sidgwick & Jackson. Special acknowledgement should also be given to *Kerrang!*, *Record Collector*, *RIP*, *Metal Gear*, *Pop Gear*, *Rolling Stone* and *Music Connection* for providing some of the source material.

And last, but hardly least, I would like to thank Slash, Duff, Axl and everybody connected with Geffen Records and the Guns N' Roses organisation for the hospitality, the turn-ons and for sharing the passing times . . .

Mick Wall, London, January 1991

INTRODUCTION

I first met the members of Guns N' Roses when I was despatched to review one of their earliest shows in Britain for *Kerrang!* magazine, in 1987. Fame hadn't yet struck – though it was plain even then that it was only a matter of time – and the band were extremely amenable. We talked in their dressing room before the show and it was agreed afterwards that we should set up a formal interview. 'Sometime over the next few days,' Alan Niven, their avuncular New Zealand-born manager assured me.

Well, the days turned into weeks and the weeks grew into months and eventually it was nearly a year later before I finally got my first interview with Guns N' Roses. Not that it mattered. It was understood early on that to expect to schedule an appointment to meet anybody in Guns N' Roses was to miss the point entirely. Like their first album, *Appetite For Destruction*, which sold over sixteen million copies worldwide, like the deaths of two fans during their ill-fated show at Donington in 1988, like the notoriety that has in the space of three short years and precisely one and a half albums turned their name into a living legend, 'it just happened', to quote the band's favourite phrase. Or didn't, as the case may be. You didn't arrange anything with Guns N' Roses any more than you arranged a good time for the sun to rise; you just had to be there.

The interviews contained in these pages, excluding the quotes in the final chapter, were conducted over a period of less than two years between 1988 and 1990. Ostensibly, they were undertaken on behalf of *Kerrang!* magazine in England and some of the material did indeed originally appear at the time in both *Kerrang!* and several other like-minded publications around the world. However, most of the material contained herein is, you can rest assured, brand new. The strictures of meeting deadlines and satisfying the demands of over-stretched sub-editors almost always means that two-thirds of the transcript of any normal ninety-minute interview will end up eating potato skins in the rubbish bin. Normally, of course, this is a good thing; most rock stars being about as articulate as the proverbial lorry.

But when it comes to someone like W. Axl Rose or Slash of Guns N' Roses – the Jagger and Richards of their generation, and particularly at the moment of birth of a brand new rock 'n' roll legend – almost everything they had to say was interesting, important and, above all, honest. That was the part that always got me the most: their over-whelming honesty. What they had to say, what they came to represent all too quickly, wasn't always pretty, but at least it was honest. In the decade that made a virtue out of greed, bullshit and self-delusion, it was the fact that when you talked to Guns N' Roses you knew they were actually telling the truth – that made what they had to say so fascinating, so peculiar and so compelling. And the truth is, if I had made up any of the stories you are about to read, nobody would have believed them.

Hence, the idea for the book you now hold in your hands. What you have here are the unedited, untrampled-on transcripts of the half dozen or so interviews it has been my fortune and my pride to have conducted with Guns N' Roses since that first tenuous meeting in England in 1987, right up to the present day – as I write, less than three months away from the release of their second album, a double, titled *Use Your Illusion*. Set within my own retelling of the extraordinary events that led up to each of those interviews, this book represents the best reasons I can put down on paper as to why I believe Guns N' Roses actually deserve the title of the Most Dangerous Band in the World.

Mick Wall, London, January 1991

The Most Dangerous Band in the World

Once in a blue moon a rock 'n' roll band will happen along that so defies the twisted logic of its times that it captures the imaginations of everybody. Not just the heavy metal hardhats, but freaks of all persuasions: from the woolly-minded rock intellectuals sipping hot toddies and wired dutifully to their Walkmans, to the seriously crazy gobblin' handfuls of speed and striking warrior poses in front of the mirror in the dead of night, on down to the little girls who like it special in a way that nobody understands.

Elvis Presley had it for a while in the fifties – one swivel of those dangerous hips guaranteed to drive the old folks crazy – before the army drilled it out of him. The Rolling Stones had it all the sixties: spiteful, hostile and as volatile as cheap whisky, they instilled fear and loathing in the hearts of all 'right thinking' citizens everywhere; qualities that turned them into idols for millions of stir-crazy teenagers the world over.

In the seventies, first it was Led Zeppelin, whose dazed and confused excesses, both musical and personal, turned their star-crossed career into a legend that continues to loom large today. And then it was the Sex Pistols. Johnny Nogood and Sidney Various. 'Anarchy in the UK' and *Never Mind the Bollocks* . . . Music to cut your wrists on. They called it punk rock but it was the same old anti-social bag of tricks: sex, drugs, violence, though not necessarily in that order. And a heightened, almost paranoiac sense of self that bordered on the psychotic.

And then, in 1987, just when we thought the whole hard rock shithouse had gone up in flames, we got Guns N' Roses – *The Most Dangerous Band in the World*, as an early headline in *Kerrang!* magazine earnestly reflected. Indeed, arriving at a time when rock 'n' roll had all but handed its balls back on a plate to the marketing moguls and media wizards of the music industry, Guns N' Roses immediately stood for everything the giants of the New Conservatism most

1

detested. They didn't respect deadlines and they didn't take advice. Worse, they admitted to drugs, swore by alcohol, and claimed not to know the meaning of the words 'safe sex'.

But then, you might ask, in the Hollyweird world of eighties-style rawk an' rawl, who did? Certainly every other LA rock band that ever copped a platinum album in the previous ten years had developed similar outre tastes. The difference was Guns N' Roses didn't lie about it. Born into a decade where, as Dr Thompson said, 'acid means rain and sex is death', Guns N' Roses were an anomaly. Thatcher's worst nightmare; Reagan's one regret. The truth was they really didn't give a fuck. And their music reflected that attitude serenely. 'You know how some bands go out and everything is going completely wrong but they can still put on a good show anyway?' Slash once tried to explain it. 'Well, we're not like that . . .'

Though its five best-known members assembled under the Guns N' Roses banner for the first time in June 1985, the origins of the band actually go back to 1982 and the arrival in Los Angeles of Jeff Isabelle and Bill Bailey; two accidents waiting to happen from Lafayette, Indiana, who were soon to rechristen themselves Izzy Stradlin' and W. Axl Rose, respectively.

Born in Lafayette on 6 February 1962, and raised as plain Bill Bailey, eldest son of L. Stephen and Sharon Bailey, 'Axl', as Slash joked back in 1986, 'is just another version of the Ayatollah'. His natural father, a notorious local trouble-maker named William Rose, had walked out on his young mother when Billy was still an infant. When his mother remarried shortly after, new husband Stephen adopted her children – Axl has a younger brother, Stuart – and gave them both his surname. Although Axl says he now looks upon his adopted father as his 'real dad', when, as a teenager, he first discovered the truth about his past he was outraged. He began to fight like a wildcat with his parents and informed all his friends that in future he should be addressed as W. Rose – the name he was indeed born with.

He was seventeen and growing his red hair long for the first time when he started thinking seriously about getting a band together. He had taken classical piano lessons as a child and had even sung in the Pentecostal church choir, and gradually he talked his way into occasional singing gigs with a succession of short-lived local Lafayette outfits. One of which was called Axl. It became his nickname – much easier than asking for W. Rose all the time – and after the band split up the name stuck.

Later on, in '86, just before Guns N' Roses signed their deal with Geffen Records, he would have his name legally changed to W. Axl

Rose. The acronym formed by the initials, WAR, he always insisted is merely coincidental, though the Lafayette police department would doubtless have something to say about that. His teenhood was fraught with head-on collisions with authority.

'I got thrown in jail over twenty times, and five of those times I was guilty,' he revealed in an early interview. His crimes: 'public consumption' and 'disturbing the peace', mostly, he said. 'The other times I was busted 'cos the cops hated me.' Indeed, Axl ended up in court so many times he took to defending himself at his own hearings because, he claimed, 'I didn't trust the public defenders for shit.' A rash course, in retrospect; he served time at various weekend 'correction centres' and was once jailed for three months when he didn't have the money to pay his latest fine.

Whichever way you looked at it, he was a reprobate. He was inspired but hard to get along with. Izzy said he remembered Axl as 'a serious lunatic when I met him. He was just really fuckin' bent on fighting and destroying things. Somebody would look at him wrong and he'd just start a fight. If it wasn't for the band, I just hate to think what he'd have done.'

Years later, Axl was diagnosed by doctors in LA as suffering from a manic-depressive disorder, a clinical condition said to be prevalent in individuals of exceptional talent. That fact alone was of little comfort to him. The doctors prescribed liberal doses of Lithium. Axl thought it was the doctors who should be taking the Lithium. 'I went to a clinic thinking it would help my moods,' he explained to Del James in *RIP* in 1989. 'The only thing I did was take one 500-question test – you know, filling in these little black dots. And all of a sudden I'm diagnosed manic-depressive! Let's put Axl on medication . . .' Except the medication didn't work, he said. 'The only thing it does is help keep people off my back 'cos they figure I'm on medication,' he chuckled darkly.

Jeff Isabelle – 'Izzy' to his friends that wanted to stay his friends – was born in Lafayette on 8 April 1962. The only member of the band to graduate from high-school with a diploma, Izzy wasn't born to the life of the itinerant rock 'n' roller; he picked up a guitar and chose it. Very much the cynic of the band, where Axl could be all fire and righteous loathing, Izzy was the kind of guy that liked to slip in and out of a room unnoticed, unobtrusive as a shadow.

Quieter than Axl, though no less intense, the two forged a familial bond early on that remains firm to this day. 'The fact that I'm from Indiana has no business being in my career,' Izzy once complained. 'It's a worthless fuckin' place.' When, in 1982, Izzy started making tracks for California, Axl was quick to follow suit. The idea was to start a band. But first they had to deal with simply being there. 'I remember for two years standing at the Troubadour and nobody talked to me,' Axl recalled. 'I didn't know what to say to them either, so you just watched and learned for a long, long time . . .'

They slept on floors and lived off the favours of a succession of girlfriends who kept them fed and handed over a little money occasionally. The first band they tried to get off the ground was called simply Rose, and featured Chris Weber who co-wrote 'Anything Goes' that would later appear on the first Guns N' Roses album. But with little real equipment and even less expertise gigs were hard to come by, and despite a change of name to Hollywood Rose the band eventually disintegrated. In 1984, Izzy briefly joined London, another band then beginning to make a name for themselves on the close-knit Hollywood club circuit, while Axl temporarily teamed up with LA Guns, fronted by guitarist Tracii Guns. Before long, though, Axl had stolen Tracii away from his own band and persuaded Izzy back to form the first fledgling line-up of what would eventually be Guns N' Roses in March 1985. (Originally they had considered such bizarre monikers as AIDS and Head of Amazon.)

The drummer in the original line-up of Guns N' Roses, Rob Gardener, was another local LA boy well-known to the others. But the bass player, Duff McKagan, was a new face on the scene, recruited from an ad Axl had placed in the local underground press. Born Michael McKagan in Seattle, Washington, on 5 February 1965, the youngest of eight children, Duff – 'My punk name,' he once informed me, somewhat red-faced – grew up 'surrounded by music'. His father sang harmonies in a barber-shop quartet and most of his brothers and sisters could play at least one instrument. It was his brother, Bruce, himself a bass player, who taught him his first few rudimentary chords on the instrument.

Musically, punk was Duff's first love and between the ages of fifteen and nineteen he played in, by his own estimation, 'over thirty of these New Wave-type bands' in Seattle alone. Not always as a bass player, either. At different times he also tried his hand at drums and guitar. At one point he was actually on the verge of becoming the drummer in the English proto-punk band, the Angelic Upstarts. 'The band came to Seattle years ago and they crashed at the house of a friend of mine, so I got to know them,' Duff explained. 'I was playing drums at the time. Then out of the blue one day they called me from San Francisco, said they were looking for a new drummer and asked if I'd be interested.' Duff went as far as rehearsing with the Upstarts but backed out when it was pointed out that joining the band would also entail moving to live in England. 'I was shit-scared of making such a jump back then,' he admitted. 'So I turned 'em down and stayed with the band I was with.'

But not for long. Still only twenty years old but already a veteran of and 'bored shitless' by the limited Seattle scene, Duff decided it was time to strike out on his own somewhere new and more promising – specifically, Los Angeles.

This decision prompted a return to the bass. Recently, Duff had been making it as a guitarist again. But, as he recalled years later, 'I had heard all these stories about LA, you know, that there were millions of great guitar players there already. And I really didn't think I was good enough to be one of the top guys. So just to get a fuckin' foot in the door, I decided to get a bass and an amp and go down to LA that way.'

Duff was fortunate in that he had only been in town a couple of months before he answered Axl's ad for a bass player. Guns N' Roses, however, were not the first band he hooked up with after his arrival in LA. The first was a ramshackle two men and a dog outfit called Road Crew – the two men being a soft-spoken corkscrew-haired Mulatto guitarist called simply Slash, and a blond-skinned drummer with a big head and a bad mouth named Steven Adler. Road Crew were always looking for musicians because nobody except Slash and Steven ever stayed for long. Duff had been given Slash's phone number and called him up 'thinking he'd be some old punk guy with a name like that. I could barely understand him on the phone. You know how Slash talks . . . But he said their influences were Aerosmith, Alice Cooper, AC/DC, Motorhead, so I thought, cool, I'll try it out.'

Duff's 'audition' was at the coffee counter of a Jewish delicatessen called Cantners where Slash could frequently be found hanging out in those days. Duff was still very much the punk, and his hair was cut spiky-short and dyed various shades of red, black and blond. 'So I walk in there still expecting to find some old punk rock guy,' Duff said. 'Slash and Steven were there with their girlfriends and they were all completely wasted. And their girlfriends immediately thought I was a homo because of my hair . . .'

Nevertheless, neither side was exactly in a position to turn the other down and so for a short spell in the spring of 1985, Duff joined Slash and Steven's Road Crew. But with rehearsals almost as rare as actual gigs, he soon decided it was time to start scanning the Musicians Wanted sections of the music press again. Which was where he found Axl's phone number. 'That line-up was really pretty bad, though,' Duff admitted with a smile, referring to the Guns N' Roses line-up as it

5

existed when he first joined the band. 'I was beginning to wonder why I was bothering with a band that was just like all the other bands I'd been in, in Seattle.'

The turning-point came when Tracii and Rob 'pussied out' of a string of low-key West Coast dates Duff had worked hard to arrange for the band, using up favours and leaning on old connections from his Seattle scene-making days. Exasperated, and with less than seventy-two hours to go to the first date he had booked for the band in Seattle, Duff hit on the idea of bringing in his former Road Crew buddies, Slash and Steven, as last-minute replacements. They certainly weren't up to anything else at the time. 'Me and Steven were basically back to being a two-man band,' Slash recalled. 'The main problem was we'd never been able to find a singer, and when Duff called at first I went along with the idea of stealing Axl for my own band . . .' His smile said it all: fat chance.

Slash – real name, Saul Hudson – was born in Stoke-on-Trent, England, on 23 July 1965, the eldest son (Slash has a little brother, Ash) of a black American mom, Ola, and a white English dad, Tony. Both were variously connected with the music business: Tony as a graphic designer, notably for the sleeve of the 1973 Joni Mitchell album, *Court and Spark*; Ola as a clothes and costume designer (she designed the clothes for David Bowie in his first starring role in the 1975 cult movie classic, *The Man Who Fell to Earth*). It was a friend of his father's who first started calling him Slash.

'I grew up in a kind of rebellious hippy household,' he explained. 'And I was given a lot of freedom as a kid. I started saying the word "fuck" when I was, like, seven or eight years old, telling my parents to fuck off all the time. I guess some people found that shocking . . .' But for all his big talk, in truth Slash was an introverted young man who found it hard to relax in company. 'That's one of the reasons I started drinking,' he once confessed. 'If I don't have a drink I sink into myself. And I like it,' he added cheerfully. 'I like being drunk! It's a habit I picked up when I was twelve years old. It helps me, it brings me out of my shell. I can't deal with people in a social situation when I'm sober.'

Life was turned upside down for the youngster, though, when his parents' marriage began to break up. The couple separated in the early seventies and for a time he lived with his grandmother. Then, when he was eleven, his father decided to up sticks and move to California, taking Slash with him. After the relative peace and quiet of suburban England, Slash confessed he found it hard at first to adjust to his hectic new life in America. 'When I first came to LA and started school, I never really fitted in. Then when I was thirteen years old I just thought, fuck it, and didn't worry about it any more. Then all of a sudden everybody was cool and I started becoming popular. It was really strange. But I didn't really care by then because I was into hanging out by myself, ditching school and practising guitar . . .'

Because of his family's association with the music business, by the time he was a teenager Slash had amassed a huge collection of records. Not just rock, but all styles of popular music. 'I always liked music. I used to listen to The Who, Joni Mitchell, Led Zeppelin, Minnie Ripperton, the Stones, Chakka Khan, you know, *Rags to Rufus*, all that stuff. Just everything we had in there.' Despite his musical background, however, the thought of actually picking up an instrument and learning how to make the music himself had, he claimed, simply never crossed his mind. The idea came, he said, when a high-school friend, Steven Adler, showed him an electric guitar for the first time and plugged it into a small amp. 'He'd just plug in and turn it all the way up and bang on it real loud, and I was just fuckin' fascinated by it!' Fascinated enough, in fact, to go out and buy himself a 'plank of wood with a few strings on it for five bucks' and take a few elementary guitar lessons, before quitting in favour of sitting at home and playing along to his Aerosmith and Led Zeppelin albums. 'Back then I didn't know the difference between bass and lead guitar, or any of that shit. I basically chose guitar 'cos it had more strings.'

Born in Cleveland, Ohio, on 22 January 1965, but better known by his own preferred description, 'from Hollywood, born and raised in America', Steven Adler moved with his family to Los Angeles when he was a child, where he grew up the quintessential California boy; sun-streaked blond, tanned and tattooed, and with eyes as blue and vacant as the postcard sky above the Hollywood hills. And like everybody else, he wanted to be a guitar player. But when he and Slash were seventeen, Steven's playing ability was already so far behind Slash's he wisely dumped the guitar and for a brief spell fancied himself as a singer, fronting another of the one-off garage line-ups Slash was constantly tinkering with. When it was plain that wasn't working either, he took to beating on pots and pans, found he had a certain penchant for it and began saving up for his first drum-kit.

Enter rather unsteadily stage-left Road Crew. 'It was a great little band,' Slash would always insist. 'Sort of like Metallica are now but without a singer . . .'

After two days and thirty-six hours of non-stop rehearsal, Axl, Izzy, Duff, Slash and Steven loaded up a friend's car and, in June '85, set off on their first tour as Guns N' Roses. It was quickly christened the Hell Tour. About a hundred miles outside of LA, the car broke down. Undeterred, the band got out and levelled their thumbs at the highway.

'We were all standing by the side of the road dressed in our stage clothes,' Duff recalled with a laugh. 'Five guys in striped tight pants and boots out in the middle of Oregon. Then when we finally got to Seattle, we had to play on other people's equipment and we were just *wasted*. It was our first gig and we sucked really bad. But it was hilarious, too. The whole trip went from bad to worse. But the playing was coming together and we knew that if we could get through that, we could get through anything . . .'

Their first gig in LA was at the Troubadour club in West Hollywood, where they impressed the management enough to get a regular Thursday night slot, first as openers, then within a few weeks as headliners in their own right. Meantime, the band were sleeping rough in a garage-cum-rehearsal room situated along the cheaper end of Sunset Boulevard – nicknamed the Hellhouse. It was so called, Izzy later explained, because, 'It was a living fuckin' hell!'

'We tried to live on $3.75 a day,' Axl recounted, 'which was enough to buy gravy and biscuits at Denny's Deli for a buck and a quarter, and a bottle of Nightrain for a buck and a quarter, or some Thunderbird. That was it. You survived . . .' The Hellhouse didn't have a shower but that didn't matter as the rain always leaked in. It had no beds so at night they stole lumber from a nearby construction site and built a makeshift loft in which they slept, above their equipment.

Del James, a friend and fellow survivor of the Hellhouse who now writes for *RIP* magazine, remembered it well: 'Izzy used to sleep in the tiny space between the back of the couch and the wall. He'd be behind there for days sometimes. You'd just see this head appear over the back of the couch occasionally, to check out what was going on, then disappear again. I'd say, "Izzy, you OK, man?" And he'd go, "Ah, yeaahhh . . ."'

Girls, as always, played a crucial if predictably subservient role in the band's day-to-day survival. 'There was a lot of indoor and outdoor sex,' Axl reminisced. 'I used to fuck girls just so I could stay at their place,' admitted Slash. 'We sold drugs,' said Izzy matter-of-factly. 'We sold girls. We *managed*. In the beginning we'd throw parties and ransack the girl's purse while one of the guys was with her.'

The band also lived for a short time at the West Hollywood apartment of their first manager – in name if not anything else – an habitue of the LA club circuit named Vicky Hamilton, whose previous claim to fame, apart from knowing every unsigned band in Hollywood by their first names, was performing similar services for Poison in the days before they were signed. That is, feeding them, letting them crash, picking up the drinks tab occasionally, letting them use the phone, taking care of the door. In one large cramped room at Vicky's they would stash amps, guitars, clothes, bodies . . . sometimes even their own.

Late '85 to early '86 found Guns N' Roses working hard building up their reputation at notorious LA haunts like the Whiskey A-Go-Go, the Roxy, the Water Club, the Troubadour, and Scream. They would encourage other local LA bands like Jetboy, Faster Pussycat and the now reactivated LA Guns to open for them. 'It kinda created this scene,' Axl reflected fondly. 'And in that crowd we were pretty much the top draw.'

The set in those days used to begin with an intro tape of 'What's That Noise' by the Stormtroopers of Death, then the lights would flash on and the band would kick into brutal stone-faced early versions of 'Reckless Life', 'It's So Easy', 'Welcome to the Jungle', 'You're Crazy', 'Move to the City', 'Nightrain', 'My Michelle', 'Shadow of Your Love' . . . By the end of 1985 the band had fourteen original songs already written and regularly being worked into shape where it counted, live in front of an audience; the still largely unfamiliar set liberally sprinkled with adrenalin-crazed covers of Aerosmith's 'Mama Kin', Elvis' 'Heartbreak Hotel', 'Jumpin' Jack Flash' by the Stones, or Rose Tatoo's 'Nice Boys (Don't Play Rock 'n' Roll)'; anything they damn well pleased, in fact.

And the audience ate it up. 'Their audience,' explained Vicky back in '86, 'went from 150 to 700 almost overnight. And it was all word of mouth.' Which was all the encouragement the West Coast-based record companies needed to suddenly start filling up the guest lists at Guns N' Roses gigs. 'The buzz got out,' said Slash. 'And we kept getting invited out to meet these idiots from record companies. One label we were talking to, I was saying, "It sounds kinda like Steven Tyler," and the chick goes, "Steven who?" All of us just looked at each other and said, "Can we have another one of those drinks?"'

'Then they started coming to see *us*,' snorted Izzy derisively. 'They would come over to the studio and come in the alley and see drunks – there'd be one guy sittin' there with a bottle on his head – and the next thing you know we're being taken out to lunch!'

The first few weeks of 1986 saw the band dining out on the expense accounts of every major record label in Hollywood. Finally the crack Geffen Records A&R team of Tom Zutaut and Teresa Ensenat won the day when they convinced the band they would be allowed the freedom to do things their way, and Guns N' Roses signed to Geffen on 25 March 1986. An album was hastily scheduled for the autumn.

Vicky Hamilton jumped ship, or was made to walk the plank, depending on which side of the fence you were sitting on, shortly after their signing and Zutaut and Ensenat spent the next few months frantically trying to procure an experienced professional management company for the band. Amongst the many potential candidates Zutaut brought along to meet the band was Aerosmith's manager, Tim Collins, who Geffen invited along to a specially arranged showcase gig at the Roxy on Sunset. Afterwards they retired to Collins' hotel suite for a late 'dinner' and informal discussion about where they saw their future heading. Everything seemed to be going reasonably well, thought Zutaut: Izzy stayed awake, Axl wasn't rude. But when Collins retired to the bedroom to get some sleep the band carried on drinking, running up a $450 drinks bill on Collins' room tab. In the morning, the straitlaced Aerosmith manager decided he'd seen enough and announced he would pass on the deal.

Finally, in August, they signed with Alan Niven's Stravinsky Brothers management company, who also oversaw the career of another soon-to-be-platinum LA act called Great White. But even Stravinsky admitted they took the band on with some trepidation. As Niven confessed to me later, 'When I signed this band, I didn't know what to expect. When I heard the first album, I thought we'd be doing well if we sold 200,000 copies. If you'd told me there was a hit single on it I would have laughed in your face,' he added, without laughing.

Their signing to Geffen, one of the most powerful rock labels in America, brought them their first headlines in the national music press, and early quotes included such gems from Slash as: 'I don't care if you think I'm big-headed about it, but this is the only rock 'n' roll band to come out of LA that's real and the kids know it.' This was backed up by Axl's own proclamation that, 'They haven't seen anything like us in the last ten years!'

The band spent the latter part of 1986 installed behind closed doors at Rumbo Studios in Canoga Park, Hollywood, laying down the first of the tracks destined for the debut Guns N' Roses album, which they had recently decided would be called *Appetite For Destruction*. It was originally scheduled for release at the end of the year, but early sessions had to be postponed – prophetically, as future events would bear out – while Slash and Izzy took much-needed time off to try and rid themselves of the heroin habits they had furtively been nurturing for most of the year. 'There was a point where I stopped playing guitar and didn't come out for three months,' Slash later revealed. What snapped him out of it, he said, was a phone call from Duff. 'He said, "You've alienated yourself from the band." Since they're the only people I'm really close to, that really affected me, and I quit.'

Anxious not to lose the momentum that had begun to gather around the band, Geffen came up with the idea of releasing a live EP as a stop-gap until they were ready to release the first Guns N' Roses recordings proper – still some six months away yet. Entitled *Live ?!*@ Like a Suicide* and ostensibly released in a limited edition of 10,000 on the band's own Uzi Suicide label (albeit distributed through Geffen), the EP featured four of the numbers from their then current set not intended for inclusion on the forthcoming album: two of their own compositions, 'Reckless' and 'Move to the City', plus two covers, Aerosmith's 'Mama Kin' and Rose Tattoo's 'Nice Boys (Don't Play Rock 'n' Roll)'.

Recorded one steamy night at a club date in Hollywood earlier in the year and produced by the band themselves, as a first bruised statement of intent, *Live ?!*@ Like a Suicide* announced the presence of Guns N' Roses to the rock world of 1986 in the manner of a lion entering a forest full of rabbits. The biggest-selling rock album in the world that year had been Bon Jovi's *Slippery When Wet*; clean-cut, radio-friendly and about as controversial as a glass of milk, it was the apotheosis of everything the safe dollar-conscious mid-eighties hard rock scene had come to represent.

From the dumb, squalling announcement of a drunken roadie at the start of side one, 'HEY, FUCKERS! SUCK ON GUNS N' FUCKIN' ROSES!' before Steven machine-guns the band into the riff to 'Reckless Life', to the grungy power-chords that loosen the teeth on 'Mama Kin' at the end of side two, Axl berating the audience, 'This is a song about your fuckin' mother!' it was clear these boys, unlike the rest of the opposition, were working without a safety net. Preferred it that way, even. The EP was dedicated to *all the people who helped keep us alive* and the initial 10,000 copies, only a few of which made it across to Britain and Europe, quickly sold out. As Izzy commented at the time: 'We felt that all the people who saw us from the beginning should have a chance to get our early stuff on record. It's like an expensive dedication to all the kids who helped us get going when we had no money.'

The EP was also warmly reviewed by rock pundits on both sides of the Atlantic, particularly in the UK where it was regarded as the choicest slice of lowlife rock 'n' roll to emerge out of LA since Motley Crue's sleazy debut, 'Too Fast for Love', in 1981. Comparisons with

Aerosmith – inevitable, perhaps, given the inclusion of 'Mama Kin' – were rife. The band, however, took any mention of themselves and one of their great heroes in the same sentence as a huge compliment. 'What I always liked about them was that they weren't the guys you'd want to meet at the end of an alley if you'd had a disagreement,' said Axl. 'I always wanted to come out of America with that same attitude. They were the only band that the people who lived in my city in Indiana would accept wearing make-up and dressing cool . . . These people thought the Stones were fags! But everybody liked Aerosmith.'

Shortly after signing with Geffen, they had abandoned the Hellhouse for a small, beaten-up wooden bungalow off Santa Monica Boulevard. Sessions for the album wound up in time for Christmas and by the start of 1987, with the mixing now safely under way, the band began rehearsing to go back on the road again, though it wouldn't be just multiple nights at the Troubadour they had to look forward to this time. Geffen announced that the first Guns N' Roses album, *Appetite For Destruction*, would be released in July and that their first full-scale US tour would actually be preceded by three dates in England, at the infamous old Marquee club in London, on 19, 22 and 28 June.

It would be the band's first live appearance outside of America, and their reputation preceded them (along with the handy Geffen press-releases). News of their imminent arrival in Britain brought on a rash of dubious stories in the gossip pages of the UK music press. Everything from a rumour that the band had already broken up to, most worrying of all, a report that Axl had been admitted to Cedar Sinai hospital in LA, where he had undergone electro-shock treatment after being arrested in a brawl outside a club in Hollywood. 'It just happened real quickly,' he was reported as saying. 'I got hit on the head by a cop and I guess I just blacked out. Two days later I woke up in hospital . . .'

Never slow to jump on a bandwagon, Britain's tabloid press also began to get in on the act. 'A ROCK BAND EVEN NASTIER THAN THE BEASTIE BOYS IS HEADING FOR BRITAIN! shrieked a headline in the *Star*, in June. It went further: 'Los Angeles based Guns N' Roses are led by the outrageous W. Axl Rose, who has an endearing habit of butchering dogs . . . He is on record as saying: "I have a personal disgust for small dogs, like poodles. Everything about them means that I must kill them."' Heady stuff and definitely not the sort of thing your ma wants to read over her soft-boiled eggs in the morning. But wait, there was more: 'The other two members [sic] of the group are as sleazy as their crackpot leader. Guitarist Slash and bass player Duff

McKagan claim they have been on a boozing binge for TWO YEARS. Says Slash: 'When we get up in the morning our hands are shaking like windmills . . .' Axl was joking, of course; Slash merely exaggerating. But the bad-boy reputation was beginning to stick and the sense of expectancy that surrounded the prospect of their first show at the Marquee was upped appreciably.

To coincide with the dates, Geffen rush-released two tracks from the forthcoming album, 'It's So Easy' and 'Mr Brownstone', as a double A-sided single on 15 June. Four days later Guns N' Roses played their first show in the UK at the Marquee. 'It's great to be in fuckin' England, finally!' Axl greeted the audience warmly from the stage that first night, as Slash wrung the last of the life out of the snarling closing guitar lines to 'Reckless Life'. But at first the capacity Marquee crowd failed to respond in kind and a hail of spit and plastic beer glasses began to rain down on the stage as the band moved quickly into 'Out Ta Get Me'. Losing patience, Axl brought the number to a premature close and addressed the hecklers directly. 'Hey, if you wanna keep throwin' things we're gonna fuckin' leave,' he intoned in a low voice crackling with menace. 'So whaddaya think?' Another glass clattered noisily into Steven's drum-kit. 'Hey, fuck you, pussy!' he cried, pointing his finger angrily at the drunken culprit and muttering incomprehensible oaths out of range of the microphone.

By the end of the third number, the almost too aptly titled 'Anything Goes', the barrage had slowed to a trickle but the damage had been done; the concentration of both the band and the over-impatient Friday night crowd had been broken and the rest of the show, though colourful and workmanlike, failed to really ignite in the expected fashion. This was reflected in the so-so reviews that appeared a few days later and, because of the strictures of deadlines, overlooked the fact that the band's second Marquee performance three nights later had by all accounts been of a much higher calibre.

Their last night at the Marquee, Saturday 28 June, Axl dedicated 'Out Ta Get Me' to 'all the critics at the back'. Wearing a 'Fuck Dancing, Let's Fuck' T-shirt, he then went on to lead the band through their most enthralling performance yet: Slash, his face buried in a long mop of dark curls, kick-starting the riff to 'It's So Easy' with one lazy punch; Axl swaying like a cobra in the sepia footlights, eyes slitted, voice growling like a wounded bear; Izzy, Duff and Steven leaning like scarecrows into the wind of the beat, teasing out the riffs then nailing them down like dead things. For the encores they cranked out a white-hot version of 'Whole Lotta Rosie' to rival that of even hoary old AC/DC's, Slash and Duff bringing the number to a calamitous end by stage-diving into the audience. Then they raised more than a few eyebrows by doing the same to Bob Dylan's 'Knockin' on Heaven's Door', which received its first public airing at the Marquee. All three of the shows were recorded and several of the numbers from their sojourn in London ended up as B-sides and bonus tracks on a variety of twelve-inch singles and picture-discs that would ensue over the next two years.

Naturally, their week in London was not without its share of incident. Slash got drunk and caused a furore at a party to celebrate the release of *Hearts of Fire*; a new movie starring Rupert Everett and Bob Dylan. And Axl almost got arrested the night before the first show after a fracas with in-store security guards on the steps of Tower Records in Piccadilly Circus. He had gone there with Alan Niven and Tom Zutaut but was feeling weak from the combined effects of jet-lag and an antihistamine pill he had taken earlier in the evening to relieve congestion. Security got agitated when they found him sitting on the steps of the entrance to the store, head in hands, still clutching an Eagles tape he had just purchased, and demanded that he move. It doesn't take much imagination to guess at Axl's reaction and it was only the timely intervention of the smooth-talking Zutaut that prevented the guards from calling in the police after Axl had threatened to do something unpleasant to their mothers.

All in all, though, that first trip to England would be looked back on by the band as a good time in their lives: a grand adventure. More than anything, it was just such a relief to get out of LA, confided Axl, where their reputation was already beginning to crowd their personal lives. 'In LA, you look out at a crowd of 700 people and you know 300 of them! This person loves you, this one hates you and this one's mad at you because you owe him five bucks. You're mad at another 'cos he owes you twenty-five ... When I'm on stage,' he went on, 'that's when I get to take what I'm worth to the public. When I'm singing a line, I'm thinking of the feelings that made me come up with the song in the first place. At the same time, I think about how I feel singing those words now, and how those words are gonna hit people in the crowd. And that's why I might be known as histrionic, 'cos I go full out ...'

But what drove him, though? A desperate grasping for some kind of truth, perhaps, or, like the publicity blurb always hinted at, merely a plunge into out and out hedonism? The truth, said Axl, was, 'I watch MTV and it's hard not to throw shit at the TV set because it's so fuckin' *boring*. Even the bands in LA, the whole music industry ... It's new to us, this business and we meet people and they say do this, do that. And we say, fuck it, fuck *you*. Because it's just not us. We do whatever we want to do . . .'

Appetite For Destruction, the first Guns N' Roses album, was released worldwide on 31 July 1987 and immediately provided the ultimate proof that here was one LA band whose talent was bigger than the heels of their cowboy boots. It was produced by veteran studio engineer Mike Clink, who had previously pushed the right buttons on albums for Heart, Ozzy Osbourne and Survivor, amongst others, and whose two main attributes, according to Slash, were 'incredible guitar sounds and a tremendous amount of patience'. *Appetite For Destruction* contained twelve tracks of raw unbridled power. But more: it contained wit and wisdom; depth and versatility. And while much was made of the fact that the word 'fuck' appeared in the lyrics on the album more than a dozen times, few could resist the spell of lines from 'Sweet Child o' Mine'.

'Welcome to the Jungle', however, Axl's latest slant on the country boy cutting loose in the big city for the first time, which opens the album, was lifted straight from the bottom drawer. Slash's opening guitar refrain echoes like hurried footsteps down an unlit alley, Axl breathes the words *'Oh, my God . . .'* before Steven brings the hammer down with a deafening thud and the rest of the band throw their shoulders hard into *that* riff.

'It's So Easy', which followed, with lyrics co-written by a friend and co-conspirator of Axl's named Wes Arkeen, was insolent and cool. Axl gave full vent to his awesome range of vocal styles; from the deep, languid, almost spoken first verse and chorus, journeying through the gently crooning ham in the middle section, to the hysterically whining misfit spitting hate at the climax. Slash's savage yet thrillingly concise guitar fills made chop-suey of the melody, instilling it with dread.

In a lighter vein, and named after the only wine the band could afford in the days before they were signed, 'Nightrain' was more of the same; Axl all bustle and pout, Slash and Izzy trailing after him with an avalanche of sour guitar notes.

'Out Ta Get Me' was about paranoia, inspired in part, Axl admitted, by his time in correction centres and 'weekend jailhouses'. 'Mr Brownstone', with its chilling refrain, was about heroin addiction, pure and unsimple. Axl had watched first Slash then Izzy succumb to the deadly lure of junk for months at a time and, having

15

also dabbled himself, albeit more discreetly and much less frequently than his band mates, as usual he spoke from first-hand experience.

Full of idealism for an age that probably only ever existed in newspapers and bad movies, 'Paradise City', which closed side one, was also the best-crafted anthem to all-American stagecoach sensibility rock 'n' roll since Van Halen's 'Jump', and a direct silver-spurred descendant of Lynard Skynard's 'Freebird'; Slash pumping out the breaks with his knee, Axl as camp and theatrical as the Stars and Stripes themselves.

Side two opened with 'My Michelle'; ostensibly a ballad that quickly becomes a tirade, and another true story. 'I met her when I was thirteen,' explained Axl, 'and went out with her later. But we ran into a hassle and I wrote this song.' Though it was played at the tempo of an insult being flung in someone's face, 'Think About You' was actually a very pretty song; Axl ignoring the steam that usually trailed from his ears long enough to poke a small, tentative smile at the clouds. But that was as nothing compared to the track that followed, 'Sweet Child o' Mine'. The song Axl wrote for his girlfriend, Erin, the beautiful teenage daughter of fifties singing star, Don Everly, it was also destined, though they could not have guessed it then, to become Guns N' Roses first No. 1 single in America.

The self-explanatory 'You're Crazy' followed; twice the speed of the original they had sketched out at their earliest gigs, but no less menacing; the narrator searching for a love. 'Anything Goes' kept the same ferocious pace, but it was the ultimate track, 'Rocket Queen', that fittingly brought the first Guns N' Roses album to its fraught and dazzling climax; the last ace in an already loaded deck, the band simply playing out of their skins. Again, it was another from the seemingly endless file of Axl's sordid true stories. 'I'm singing as if it's me, but it's about this girl I know. I'm singing as though I was in her shoes, and then at the end of the song I'm singing the song to her. The girl it's written about, her life is history now,' he added dispassionately. 'I mean, she's alive but there's not much left of it. Since I've been in LA I've lost five or six friends that I used to hang with every day. It's a fucked thing . . .'

The reviews that greeted the release of *Appetite For Destruction* were mixed, to say the least. The dedicated rock magazines were quick to lavish praise on it but the mainstream establishment organs, as personified by the lugubrious *Rolling Stone*, either found it too bitter a pill to swallow and damned it with faint praise, or more often just ignored it completely. This was 'heavy metal' after all, wasn't it? And to be taken with a pinch of something a bit more potent than salt, ho ho ho. That is, not to be taken too *seriously* . . .

What the highbrow critics did take seriously though was the artwork for the sleeve of the album. A reproduction of a painting by American fantasy artist Robert Williams, it depicts what appears to be a robot in a long brown coat in a post-coital scene with a young woman, panties around her ankles, one breast exposed, an aghast expression on her face. The sleeve caused such consternation in the US that a new sleeve had to be quickly substituted – a plain black sleeve featuring Axl's tattoo of a death's-head cross studded with five skulls, each of which represented a different member of the band – before any of the major chains of US record stores would stock the album on their sanitized shelves. The alternative 'black' sleeve was also made available to record retailers in Britain after W H Smith banned the original sleeve from their shelves and Virgin Megastore in London refused an in-store display.

Meantime, to begin promoting the album in America, in August the band took off for a six-week tour opening for The Cult, whose singer, Ian Astbury, had offered them the gig after witnessing one of their Marquee shows. 'He spent more time in our dressing room than his own,' quipped Axl. It was a shrewd bill for the times and the Gunners went down well with The Cult's audience. But that didn't stop Axl from getting into trouble again. This time in Atlanta, where police actually walked on stage and arrested him during the second song for attacking one of the arena security guards just before the band went on. He was held for questioning backstage while the rest of the band were left to get on with their 45-minute set as best they could. A roadie hurriedly hauled on stage helped out with some of the vocals, while Slash contributed a fifteen-minute guitar solo and Steven managed a ten-minute drum solo to fill in the gaps.

After that, the plan had been to return to Britain, this time for a proper tour, opening at theatres and concert halls for Aerosmith – 'a bill made in hell!' as Slash described it in gleeful anticipation. But when the Boston banditos pulled out at the last minute and the band were suddenly left with an empty date-sheet, the bold decision was taken to go ahead with some of the dates anyway, with the Gunners headlining their own shows. Faster Pussycat, who had also released their first album that year, were roped in as support and, in October '87, Guns N' Roses arrived back in Britain for five dates; beginning at the Rock City in Nottingham and ending seven days later at the Hammersmith Odeon in London.

To keep the ball rolling, Geffen released 'Welcome to the Jungle' as a single, and Axl took up where he'd left off on tour with The Cult, ripping his phone out of the wall of his hotel room on the evening of the first show in Nottingham, and throwing it down the stairwell at the terrified receptionist. The shows themselves were equally volatile. The first night at the Rock City they had the hardcore regulars up and stamping their feet from the moment they walked on and ripped like a knife into 'It's So Easy', and kept them there, dangling like puppets, until they strode off into the wings ninety minutes and two encores later. Afterwards hundreds of over-zealous fans nearly succeeded in overturning the tour bus as it attempted to leave the hall.

At the Manchester Apollo the following night, however, most of the audience remained in their seats throughout the show and the balcony area was closed off due to lack of ticket sales. Tellingly, that night the show lasted a little over sixty-five minutes, including the solitary half-hearted encore. Attendances for the shows on the whole were good, if not great. But by the time the tour reached the Hammersmith Odeon the band were less than 200 tickets short of a sell-out. The band responded by turning on one of their most exciting performances of the tour. They played most of the new album, of course, plus a selection of their by now familiar covers. But the highlight, for me anyway, was 'Rocket Queen'.

Live, the band extended the already lengthy six-minute album version by another five minutes or so. Halfway through the song, just as Slash came to another back-arching run across the frets, one boot resting easy on a monitor, Steven's drums began a long death-rattle beat, the guitars winked out and the band faded into the wings, the drums taking over. Then Izzy reappeared by Steven's side on the drum riser, a pair of sticks in his hands, and began hammering home some beats of his own. Suddenly Duff was there too, on the opposite side of the drums, taking his turn at rapping it out on a pair of snares. Then Axl came swaggering out of the shadows, tugging at Duff's bass, and Slash sidled back into the spotlight stage-centre and let it all come down in a shit-rain of bad-intentioned guitar notes that sent a cold sweat running down my back. It was a supreme moment and the proof, if any were really needed, that Guns N' Roses didn't need the cloistered in-bred atmosphere of a club to work their magic in. These fuckers could do it anywhere. The message seemed to be: the bigger the crowd, the bigger the band, the bigger the bang when the two met head-on.

'Welcome to the Jungle' followed, receiving the biggest cheer of the night, and 'Paradise City' ended the set in fine high-stepping style. The first encore, 'Knockin' on Heaven's Door', Axl dedicated to the memory of Todd Crew, a young friend of the band's who had occasionally roadied for them over the years. That is, when he wasn't working on keeping up his heroin habit. Indeed, Todd had accompanied them to London for their Marquee shows four months before when, unable to score, he drank himself into unconsciousness and missed the whole of the first show. Back in LA before The Cult dates, they had tried to persuade him to seek medical help for his problems. But between then and their return six weeks later, in September, he had tragically died from a heroin overdose. As always, Axl took his stance straight from the eye of the hurricane. At the very peak of the frenzy, he was there to calmly remind us of the things most of us would prefer not to know about; the lone voice that cries out in the darkest hour before the dawn.

Guns N' Roses had entered Britain with the image of dog-killing, drug-dealing, booze-sodden monsters that feasted on babies for breakfast and spat out the bones. But they left, though it wasn't yet reflected in record sales, with a growing reputation as one of the foremost rock 'n' roll noise-making machines on God's earth. The Most Dangerous Band in the World had well and truly arrived. The rest, they decided, should be candy. All they had to do now was hang on.

TWO

Welcome to the Jungle

JUNE 1988

If Los Angeles ain't the epitome of Paradise City, then tell me – where is? The richest city in the wealthiest state of the most powerful nation on earth, it even has the best climate – once the sun's burned off the early morning smog, that is. LA is Tinsel Town run amok, Sodom and Gomorrah on a skateboard. Where the billboards dwarf the buildings (big on the hoardings along Sunset Boulevard this month were *Rambo III* and *Crocodile Dundee II*) and the sculpted beauty of ninety per cent of the female population can block out every thought in your head. LA is also, of course, the home of Guns N' Roses, and I was looking forward to seeing the band in action on their own turf. Since we had last met in England, eight months before, the band's career had begun to skyrocket. Straight after the last English date they had returned to America and hooked up with their biggest, most prestigious tour yet: replacing Whitesnake as the opening act for Motley Crue.

At that time – late '87 – Motley were at the very height of what bass player Nikki Sixx would later disingenuously refer to as the band's 'bad boy period'. On paper, the combination of Motley Crue and Guns N' Roses ripping it up on the road together was a heady prospect. And so it proved in the flesh, the two bands competing relentlessly with each other for the title of truly, the most dangerous band in the world. And not just on stage, either. Every night after the show the two bands would hang out together. A particularly unholy alliance was formed between Slash, Nikki Sixx and Steven Adler, who would go out together each night and cause utter mayhem in whatever bar of whatever unfortunate Midwestern town the tour happened to be in at the time. The team only broke up after Steven fractured his hand in a nasty bar-room brawl (Cinderella drummer Fred Coury was hastily drafted in for the remainder of the dates) and Slash was officially warned by the Crue's management that the Gunners would be off the tour if he didn't curtail his after-midnight activities with the wayward Motley bass player forthwith.

Which he did – for about forty-eight hours. (The real break up of the team only occurred after Nikki OD'd on heroin one night. Slash and Steven discovered Nikki comatose on the floor of his hotel room. Slash called the paramedics while Steven dragged the unconscious body into the shower and turned on the cold water. Without their timely intervention it is doubtful Nikki would still be alive today.)

Back in LA at the start of '88, the band began to plan their own headlining tour of America: not of arenas – not yet – but of the kind of theatres and large halls they had performed in as support on The Cult's tour. Current UK flavour of the month, Zodiac Mindwarp, were signed on as special guest, with German sheet-metallists, Udo, booked as the opening act. To kill time until the tour began, the band re-entered Rumbo studios with producer Mike Clink and cut a string of acoustic-based numbers: 'Patience', 'One in a Million', 'Used to Love Her', 'Corn Chucker' and a slow sinister reworking of 'You're Crazy' from the *Appetite For Destruction* album. These were recorded mostly 'live' in the studio, and were originally intended to be used as 'future B-sides, or possibly an EP', as the Gunners said whenever anybody asked.

With *Appetite For Destruction* now beginning to accelerate up the U.S. album charts – it was then Top Twenty and rising rapidly – almost all the dates for the forthcoming tour had already sold out by the time the band hit the road in March. Back out on tour, controversy continued to trail after them like a dog on the scent of a familiar old bone: Axl was arrested trying to smuggle a Sten-gun across the Canadian border; Slash and Duff were arrested for more brawling in a bar in Seattle. And then the ultimate: a fortnight before the end of the tour, Axl walked out of the band after a violent bust-up in his hotel room one night.

It was the first time anything like that had happened – though it would not be the last – and at first the other band members were stricken. However, as we now know, Axl was back in the band after he spoke to Slash on the phone three days later. Like a couple that sadly announces their separation to all and sundry then gets back together again the very next night, both Axl and the band were mostly embarrassed by the whole thing and refused to say any more about it in public. In private, heads would be shaken resignedly and the by now well-worn expression, 'Well, you know Axl . . .' would be used to sum up their feelings.

They continued with the tour which ran through to the end of April,

21

after which the band had originally planned to get back onto the U.S. arena circuit with the special guest spot on the latest David Lee Roth tour. But somewhere in there amongst the din of clashing egos the idea was eventually abandoned and, in May, Guns N' Roses set out on the road again opening the show at arenas for Iron Maiden. 'Sweet Child o' Mine' was released as a single to coincide with the dates and it slammed its way almost immediately into the U.S. Top Forty – it looked like Guns N' Roses were about to have their first big hit single. Indeed, 'Sweet Child o' Mine' was destined to become the band's first major worldwide hit. (To capitalise on its success in Japan, the Tokyo branch of Geffen released a one-off mini-album entitled *Live From the Jungle*, featuring the album version of 'Sweet Child o' Mine', plus live versions of 'Whole Lotta Rosie', 'Knockin' on Heaven's Door', 'Shadow of Your Love' and 'It's So Easy', recorded at the '87 London Marquee shows, and 'Move to the City', culled from the original *Live ?!*@ Like a Suicide* EP, and a Japanese tour was swiftly slotted in for July.)

Meantime, the Iron Maiden tour was not going as well for Guns N' Roses as had been expected. The chief problem, it seemed, was that Maiden had experienced unexpected difficulty selling tickets for some of the earlier dates on the tour. Now, with the added spice of the most dangerous band in the world on the bill, suddenly they were starting to play to packed houses again and the feeling grew inside the Guns N' Roses camp that it was they and not Iron Maiden who should be headlining their own tour. So unimpressed were the band by their new tour-mates, in fact, that Duff even took a week off from the tour to fly back to LA and marry his longstanding girlfriend, Mandy, leaving his pal, former Cult bassist, Kid Chaos – these days known simply as Haggis – to fill in for him.

By the time I caught up with the tour in June – I had planned to see Guns N' Roses opening for Maiden over two nights at Irvine Meadows, a 17,000-capacity outdoor amphitheatre in Long Beach, California – things had degenerated to the point where the two bands were hardly speaking to each other.

And then at the last minute, to add injury to insult, the Guns N' Roses camp announced that they would be forced to pull out of the remainder of the Maiden dates after Axl – who had been losing his voice periodically throughout the tour – had been ordered to his bed by his doctors. The diagnosis: nodules on the vocal chords, a painful condition familiar to people who scream their lungs out for a living, for which the only known cure is complete rest, or if that fails, surgery. Unfortunately, like a lot of other people there that night, I didn't find any of this out until I was already at the venue. Slash was the one who broke the news to me. 'Ah, man, it's fucked.' He threw up his hands. 'The guy's not even allowed to speak. Can you imagine that – Axl not being able to open his mouth?' he shook his head in awe.

Ironically, the band drafted in to replace Guns N' Roses on the bill were LA Guns. As a gesture to try and appease the disappointed Guns N' Roses fans there, Slash and Duff got up and jammed with LA Guns the first night. The following night the whole band – minus Axl, of course – got up straight after LA Guns had finished their set and bolted through an impassioned if ramshackle version of 'It's So Easy' with Duff handling lead vocals. 'I was never so fuckin' scared in all my life!' Duff declared afterwards, still visibly quaking.

With the band temporarily off the road, Slash – who had had no permanent home for the past year, he explained – had taken a room at the Continental Hyatt House on Sunset, which, as chance would have it, was practically opposite the hotel I was staying in at the time, Le Mondrian. The two of us agreed to get together over the coming days and talk. 'I'm staying under the name of Mr Disorderly,' he smirked. 'Gimme a call . . .' A couple of days later I did.

The popularly received image of the Guns N' Roses guitarist – the mane of long, tangled dark curls falling past his shoulders and hiding his face; the slightly swaying presence in the top hat, cut-down Led Zeppelin T-shirt, tight-arsed black jeans and scuffed cowboy boots, pulling on a bottle of Jack Daniels and peeling out one dirty riff after another like he could do it blindfolded – is real enough all right not to be called a pose. But there are still some things about Slash that the videos, the record sleeves and the magazine pin-ups don't tell you. The sort of stuff that simply doesn't register on a colour transparency or the shiny surface of a CD.

His speaking voice, for example: it's soft, quiet, never finding a reason to raise itself too far above the comforting clink and rattle of glasses being drained in a bar. When Slash talks, which he likes to do a lot, he keeps his conversation lucid but cool, warm without fumbling, setting his cards down carefully on the table. And no, he doesn't walk around all the time with an open bottle of Jack jammed in his fist. Only most of the time. He's working on it, though . . .

'The afternoon we found out we would have to quit the Maiden tour I went around grabbing every bottle of Jack I could find stashed around our dressing room and took it all back to the hotel,' he told me. 'That was five days ago and I've been living off it ever since. But now I'm down to my last bottle and a half. After that, I guess I'll be back to buying my own,' he said with an air of comic dismay, meaning it, not meaning it. 'It'll be the first time I've had to go out to a liquor store for my own booze in ages . . . Maybe I won't remember how to do it,' he tittered.

A kid but not a kidder, beneath the fell-out-of-bed hair and the whiskey smile, there was something far less relaxed going on. At twenty-two, Slash already had the demeanour of an old hand at this game he was in. He knew enough already, it seemed, to blithely dismiss the astonishing success his band had enjoyed over the previous twelve months with a nonchalant wave of the arm. 'Oh, man, what do I want to know about all that for? Sure, I like it that we're going places, doing things and being allowed to play and make the kind of records we want to. Beyond that, all you can talk about is money, and that's where I get lost . . .' He rolled his eyes.

'I mean, look at me – T-shirt, jeans, boots, that's me, that's all there is, that's all there's ever gonna be. I don't even like the idea of going into a fuckin' dressing room and changing into different clothes just to go on stage and play. Gimme a roof over my head and something to drink and I've got everything I need. What difference is this money going to make?'

I was tempted to answer that one for him, but I figured he'd find out for himself soon enough.

The afternoon Slash and I got together to tape this interview, it was typical Los Angeles summer weather: the sun boiling like an egg in the blue saucepan sky; an endless stream of traffic dragging its aching gears up and down Sunset; the sidewalks empty save for me and Slash and the other West Hollywood bums. The previous evening Slash had dragged me against my will to a party which LA Glamsters, Poison, were throwing over at a dive called the London Club. 'Come on, man, let's go and start a fight!' he had laughed at me. 'I'll take care of you . . .'

The much-publicised animosity that existed then between Guns N' Roses and the members of Poison went back a long way. One of the stories goes that in the days before Guns N' Roses, Slash actually passed an audition to join Poison in the spot guitarist CC DeVille now occupies, but turned the gig down when he realised they'd expect him to dye his hair blond and daub his face in the heavy make-up that was soon to become Poison's trademark. 'Fuck that,' Slash hissed, when I reminded him of it. 'I didn't want to look like a clown . . .'

Slash also told me that in the early days before either band had secured a recording contract, Guns N' Roses and Poison would occasionally appear together on small club dates in LA. 'Some nights they'd come on first, some nights we would,' he recalled. 'It really didn't matter, neither of us had a really big following yet. A lot of people would come down just to see what was going on and then split.

'But every time those assholes played first, Bret Michaels would end their set by announcing that the band were having a big party somewhere and everybody was invited. And, man, the people who frequent the sort of dives we were playing in those days didn't need to be asked twice to go to some party, and within minutes the fuckin' club would be empty! They were always pulling sneaky, shitty little stunts like that. And that kind of attitude sucks, man . . . I think it's because they're insecure about their talent.'

Slash said he felt particularly irked when, some months later, after both bands had been signed and released albums, CC DeVille took to wearing a top hat on stage at Poison concerts. 'Listen, I'm not saying I was the first rock 'n' roller to wear a top hat on stage. But look, man, CC is the type of guy who probably didn't even know what a top hat was until he saw me wearing one. You know, I caught up with him one night in the Rainbow, and I just told him quietly, "If I ever see you wearing a top hat on stage again I'm gonna shoot you . . ." I tell ya, he freaked, man!' Slash bawled with laughter. 'And, I mean, I don't own a gun . . . wouldn't know how to use one if I did. And I'm really not a violent guy at all. I just felt something had to be said. Sometimes you gotta draw the line for people.'

So anyway, we went to the party, but apart from a few chaste exchanges between Slash and Bret Michaels, nothing much occurred. No fights, no real tittle-tattle. Slash's bottle of Jack looked like it was doing all right, though; as the guitarist crash-danced he swirled it around by the neck, then when he slumped up against a wall he cradled it in his arms like a baby.

Walking up Sunset towards my hotel the following afternoon, Slash was looking good for an apprentice vampire: tired red eyes hidden behind stark mirror-shades, only mild shakes – a long sloping shadow looking for the right doorway to duck into. We settled ourselves in the shade of the poolside bar at Le Mondrian and ordered Jack Daniels and beer chasers. Out in the sun, belly-flopped on towels beside the pool, were a gaggle of teenage girls, all of whom had spotted the tall, rangy guitarist the moment he strolled in and dropped his body into the nearest empty chair. Two or three of them tiptoed over to where we were seated and pressed their faces up against the glass partition separating the bar from the pool. Slash appeared not to notice. 'Well, man, where do we begin?'

By asking for an update on the news about Axl's damaged voice, I suggested?

'I'm no doctor,' he said, lighting a Marlboro. 'But what it is, he's got nodules on his vocal chords and he can't hit a certain range – which is his whole high voice. The chords crowd each other because of these bumps or nodules or whatever. So he just can't sing right now. It got to the point on stage where it just sounded awful. Trying to sing 'Knockin' on Heaven's Door', or one where he really screams it, he would get to this note and just go. It was like, where's he going? It was like no key at all, it was really strange.

'We did a date with Maiden in Palo Alto which was really bad, to the point that I was having to do guitar solos to fill the space 'cos Axl couldn't sing. So he went to the doctor there and the rest of us drove to the next gig in Sacramento and set up our equipment. We sound-checked, everything sounded great. We were waiting for Axl to show up when our road manager gets this phone call saying that not only is Axl not going to be able to make the gig, but they didn't think he'd be able to finish the tour!

'The fucking thing is, what they did was go back out after the doors had been opened, after our banner was up on stage and everything, and start taking off the gear. The kids saw the gear going off and started freaking out. I had to go out in front of, I think it was like 22,000 kids, and go, "Axl's voice isn't working right at the moment, we're not going to be playing tonight." They just went nuts! Then Axl showed up about ten minutes later and we drove straight to LA.

'Since then he's seen another doctor here in LA who says the problem with Axl's voice has been developing for a long time. So he's going for a final opinion on Tuesday and we'll know then if we're going to Japan at the end of the month or not.'

How long would they have to wait for Axl's voice to heal?

'If he has to have surgery, we have to wait a week for the swelling to go down before he has the surgery. Then we have to wait for that to heal. We're looking at about two weeks – if the operation goes well and Axl stays out of trouble,' he added meaningfully. 'Basically, we have three months on the Aerosmith tour coming up, so I don't want anything to fuck up that. Of all the tours we'll have done in the last year – besides the Monsters of Rock thing in England which we're doing this year – that is the tour for us. Us and Aerosmith – that is really a great combination for a live show, doncha think?'

Undeniably, I told him, blinking just at the thought of it.

'Man, if I was a kid and going to see a concert that would be the fucking one! I'm really looking forward to it . . . There's one gig we're playing on that tour, at the Giants Stadium in New York – it's Aerosmith, Deep Purple and us. Fucking monster gig!'

Why not? Guns N' Roses were, after all, rapidly turning into a monster band.

'I know,' said Slash, hooded eyes staring blankly past my shoulder, his thoughts turned momentarily inward. Had it affected him, though, the huge, still-burgeoning success of the band and the constant high-profile attention that came with it?

'I don't feel any different but I get a lot more attention thrown my way,' he said. 'Mostly 'cos I do all our press most of the time, so everybody is familiar with mc. I have to take a security guard with me when I'm on the road now, though, 'cos they're scared I'm gonna die, or something. It's sort of embarrassing 'cos nobody can just walk around and hang out with you or whatever. So it's a drag in that sense, but it's also cool because when a flock of people come up and they all want autographs, I don't have the personality to just say fuck off. So he'll keep them off my back and make sure it doesn't get out of hand.'

How about the business side of things: did Slash try and keep up with all the latest sales figures and all that?

'We get all these phone calls – yesterday it was 35,000 record sales, today it's 91,000 sales and we just got a breaker on the single . . . It freaks my ass out! So I guess you could say that we are turning into what you'd call a big band. I think the thing for me, though – what would really solidify it for me – would be to do the next record and see where that one goes. If we've done two albums and we're still going on that steady uprise kinda thing, that would be cool. The material for the next record, by the way, is great . . .' he confided.

Though it would be another three years before the next full-length Guns N' Roses album would finally be released – not that Slash or anybody else could have known that then – back in June '88, Slash claimed the band already had 'lots of new songs' written.

'We've been writing on the road. How it works is, I write a lot of the guitar parts and chord changes and the so-called bitchin' riffs, and Izzy writes real good rock 'n' roll chord changes, you know what I mean? Then Axl gets pissed off at something and starts writing words. He gets these melodies and these rhythms happen. Like, he'll take me into the shower at the gig and say listen to this and start singing something he's just made up.

'It looks like it's gonna be really good, too. It looks like it's gonna be even more angry and anti-radio and stuff. The first album, everybody was shocked by it 'cos it said "fuck" on it, like, twenty-five times. This one could be even worse. The subject-matter on this one is a little more . . .' He paused mid-sentence to summon the cocktail waiter over and order himself another double Jack, then lost the thread.

I asked for the names, maybe, of some of the newly finished songs.

Slash scraped at the stubble on his chin with the back of his hand and admitted that he wasn't too hot on actual titles. 'I don't really concentrate on the lyrics until we're actually putting the shit down in the studio. I have to sit with Axl and see what the reality of the album is gonna be about.' But he managed to pull a couple of names out of the hat. 'There's one called "Perfect Crime". Another called "You Could Be Mine" . . . Hey, that rhymes! And that's about all I can remember right now.'

The conversation moved on to the slow but inexorable rise of the current Guns N' Roses album in the U.S. charts. Almost a year to the day since its release, *Appetite For Destruction* had just entered the *Billboard* Top Ten for the first time. (Less than two months later it would be No. 1 and remain there or thereabouts for the rest of the year.)

Slash said he thought it was 'the perfect way for a first album to happen. To me, it would be a great disappointment for it to come out and the record company ship, say, 500,000, so it jumps into the charts at fifty-something and then a week later it's gone. It was the opposite for us. We went in the *Billboard* Top 200 at, like, 168 or something, and from there it just kept steadily climbing. The greatest thing for me was seeing it go from one side to the other – going into the Top Fifty.'

What about when *Appetite* sold its first million: that must have been a rare kind of thrill, to be told the first record you'd ever made had just sold a million copies?

'At first, I didn't really know,' he said evenly. 'I'm pretty naïve about all this stuff. I try to keep my wits about me in most things. But in this whole band there's a certain naïvety in the way we approach this whole business. When we went out in the beginning, it was like, we're a rock band and we don't know about any other shit. But we were playing so we knew how to book a gig. Then it was like, there's all these record companies who want to sign us and our attitude was, well, fuck 'em. We're only gonna sign to the one who gives us what we want.

'So we went with Geffen and the next thing is we're gonna go on tour, on the Cult tour. I was like, wow, the Cult tour! It must be huge! Then six months later we were going out headlining the same places those guys were when we were backing them. Then it was, ah, I guess they weren't really all that big, were they? Now it's moved up another gear again and recently we've had promoters coming up to us and saying, "You guys shouldn't be opening for Iron Maiden, 'cos you could headline here."' He sat back and lit another cigarette. Inhaled, exhaled. Then shook his head and said he still found it hard to take in – the acclaim, the attention, the album sales that were now beginning to be counted in millions. 'The concept of us headlining somewhere like the [13,000-capacity] LA Forum – I can't swallow that. But the promoters risk a lot of money booking tours and if they want to do that maybe they know what they're talking about, who knows?'

How did Slash think Guns N' Roses would adjust to headlining for the first time at a giant American arena – was it an intimidating prospect?

'No, it's the greatest,' he replied, no hesitation at all. 'Headlining is always the best. You've got lots of stage space. I'm all over the place, I can go nuts. And we don't have to worry about keeping the set tight as far as, *vroom vroom vroom*, song after song so you can squeeze it all in. We can go out and play for two, two-and-a-half hours. That's comfortable for us.

'I mean, when we're on stage, that's us, on tour. It's like, all this work is geared to that forty-five minutes on stage. If we had two hours it would just be better. It would just be the best and I can't wait. But first we gotta get another album out . . .'

And then I asked it. The question I would find myself repeating in every subsequent interview I would conduct with the members of Guns N' Roses: 'When do you actually expect to start recording the next album?'

I even believed Slash – I think he may even have believed it himself at the time – when he replied earnestly, 'We're gonna go into the studio in, like, October, November . . .' It seems risible now, of course, but at that point Slash said he believed the next album would be in the stores sometime in mid-1989. He even said he knew what he'd like to see the band doing after its release. 'When the next one comes out then hopefully, if the spirit's there, we'll do a lot of summer outdoor concerts and festivals. We'd do that as a support, I guess, on a big bill like the Monsters of Rock thing. Then after that, go out and start headlining. And then I never want to open for anybody ever again,' he said cheerfully, reaching for his glass.

I asked if headlining at arenas would mean the band having to change their act in any way. How did Slash think the essentially club-style live Guns N' Roses experience – earthy, lurid, just one punch away – would translate over the wide-screen expanse of 20,000 people? Would they be tempted into going for one of those huge,

29

spare-no-excess production numbers favoured by more 'wordly' contemporaries like Iron Maiden, Bon Jovi, Motley Crue, and the rest of the spangly gang?

He pulled a face. 'Well, you know, we're not really like that. I mean, my attitude is basically, fuck changing clothes to go on stage, I'm just gonna put on my jeans. My feeling about it is, if you can't go out and kick ass, if you have to have stage props and lighting effects and this and that and the other, it's probably because you can't do it as a band. Like, Maiden is a good band, I guess, I don't know, I'm not really into Iron Maiden. But if you strip them of . . .' he paused, then changed his mind. 'No, actually, I can't say that about Maiden, 'cos they have done that – they've done plenty of club gigs. OK, strike that one.

'But there are a lot of bands that couldn't just go out and strip away all that shit and kick ass. They get better every year 'cos their stage set gets bigger every year. Some bands it's like they went out and bought the clothes first and then decided to start thinking about the music.' He snorted derisively. 'That's what we're really against. I know it's a cliché but there are bands out there whose roots go back about three years, you know what I'm saying? It's ridiculous, there's no soul in it, there's no dynamics in the music or anything. It's just bland. They pick up a 4/4 beat and then it chugs away and then that's it. But they look good. We're just gonna go out and we'll have a backdrop that says "Guns N' Roses", right? And just hammer our amps and just go out and play . . .'

We got onto the thorny subject of MTV. In the for and against debate, Slash said he was most definitely against – this despite the fact that MTV were then airing the 'Sweet Child o' Mine' video twice an hour, every hour, twenty-four hours a day, with the result that the single was now rising rowdily towards the No. 1 spot in the U.S. charts (though at the time we spoke that particular milestone was still a month or so away).

'Yeah, I know, but whether MTV played our videos or not it wouldn't change a fuckin' thing about the way we play our music or why we play our music. But a lot of bands, you ask who their main influences are, if they were honest they should say MTV. Think of the future,' he said, trying to attract the attention of the cocktail waiter again. 'It's gonna be sick,' he continued. 'There's gonna be kids out there reminiscing over the last Poison video. Sad . . . The only effect I can think of that really enhances a rock show is really dramatic lighting, just to set moods. But all the other stuff is just bullshit. I don't have the patience for it, my attention span is not that long. I couldn't sit at a drawing table with the guys in the band and some execs and a couple of mindless painters going, "Duhhh . . . how's that?" We just wouldn't be able to do it. We're incapable of it.'

But surely, I wondered, wouldn't the fact that Guns N' Roses' music was now being rotated so heavily on MTV have a balancing effect on the audience: prove to them that there was life beyond the next Poison video, after all?

'Hopefully. But what you're looking at mostly, as far as I'm concerned, is this middle-class kid coming up into this corporation type deal and watching all the changes that happen. Everything flies by him and it's like, "Wow, check this out!" Except it doesn't really mean anything. But I go out to clubs when I'm on the road and I see bands playing our songs. I got up one night with a band who did "Paradise City" – completely wrong, on top of it!' he grinned. 'But I thought, that's great, you know? I'm hoping people will be influenced by us because, whatever our image, whatever people see in us to make us as big as we are, I hope it's more because we persevere, because we're sincere and that we honestly get down and play and really try to be good. I would hope that that was what set the standard.'

But what if they did it for all the wrong reasons? Imitation is cheap whether it's of Guns N' Roses or anybody else.

'If people start going around in cowboy boots and top hats and still don't give a shit how they play and just want to look like us, then obviously that's totally a piece of shit. I'd feel real disappointed, I'd feel that I didn't accomplish much.'

But what about the other side of the band's image, the fuck-you attitude behind the funky clothes. Was Slash aware how nervous some people got when the band walked in the room?

'Good,' he chuckled. 'There's a lot of that goes on, yeah. Oh God, Slash is here, or Axl is here, they're gonna smash the place up . . . But you know, you've been with me. I'm not that bad a guy. I'm sort of boisterous sometimes.' He smiled disingenuously. 'The only time I ever use it, though, is on the fuckin' assholes out there who try and fuck with you. It's the same thing as being eaten by a wolf – we smell the fear. So we fuck with people sometimes. But I don't go out of my way just to be . . . I'm not one of those guys who sits there with this complex and goes out and . . . That kind of shit happens because people ask for it. They ask you dumb questions and shit and that just pisses me off.'

Slash began to talk of anti-heroes; villains that became champions and blazed a trail that could never be erased from his mind, even if some of the best of them were now dead, and the best of the rest had long since begun to fade.

'I used to dig The Who a lot, I still dig Pete Townshend a lot. He's still got that nihilistic attitude. But the Stones as a band and as individuals is the shit that we grew up with. The seventies stuff. We happened to choose the more decadent shit. That was what was cool. Keith Richards was great . . . Jimmy Page, though, is the guy who I have listened to incessantly for the longest time. He can't go on stage and play a note these days, but he's still great,' he twinkled wickedly.

I commented that for a lot of people Slash exuded some of the same charisma on stage as a Richards or Page; that the audience might easily spend just as much time ogling him as Axl, his frontman. It was the classic textbook rock partnership – Mick and Keef, Robert and Jimmy . . . Axl and Slash.

'Really?' he looked genuinely surprised.

'You know, you're the classic head down, no shit, bad man on guitar, aren't you?' I teased.

'It's some aggressive shit going out there all right,' he agreed. 'I will see photos and I will watch video tapes of the band, and I see different things in it. I see me as sort of off the wall, like, here, there, here, there. Smoking and throwing up and shit. But Axl, if you really watch Axl, he's got this really intense presence, very cool. Then there's Duff . . . he's real tall and he'll have his bass real low. Every time he stands, his steps are like this far apart, and he goes "Grrrrr!" Duff's great, I crack up when I watch him on stage. Then there's Izzy, who's just sort of like . . . in the background most of the time. And Steven . . . Steven is like one of those David Lee Roth types . . . Whenever I watch the band I always think there are lots of things to keep your attention. It's all ridiculous, it's like a circus, you know?'

And yet, the band always appeared as though it was on the verge of falling apart. It had, in fact, become a big part of Guns N' Roses' appeal, hadn't it?

Slash nodded his shaggy mane and slurped noisily at his drink. 'I'd rather it collapsed,' he stated flatly. 'This might sound sort of negative, but I'd rather be as good as possible in the amount of time that you can do it, and do it to the hilt. Then fall apart, die, whatever. I'd rather do that than do five or six albums, ten albums, and end up like Kiss.'

Except that most of their fans now seemed more concerned that Guns N' Roses might not even get around to making a second album, let alone a fifth or sixth. Axl, for example, had already left the band once . . .

'That was no big deal,' Slash insisted. 'Except when you cancel a gig it starts this whole big upheaval. Everyone freaks out and the press plays up about it. We weren't scared that the band was gonna fall apart, we were pissed off at Axl. But we sat down and talked about it over a couple of beers and everything was fine.'

Axl, it was said, could be a notoriously 'difficult' character to deal with. I asked how the two of them got along as people outside the band?

'We love each other,' said Slash unequivocally. 'The whole band . . . we're, like, real tight, so that kind of fear of someone leaving is not in the back of my head all the time. I don't worry about it. It's like, I would only worry if something happened to them, you know? 'Cos I couldn't continue this band minus one of these guys. The whole reason this band works is because of the chemistry between the five of us. We aren't what you'd call superior musicians or anything like that, but we work within the framework of Guns N' Roses. It's like, Steven changes the dynamics of the song and I know how to play with that. I know how it works. I'm used to playing with these guys, you know? I have a real strong bond with all of them. We have our fights and arguments but I wouldn't try and stick somebody else in the middle of all this shit. Are you kidding?' he joked, a wan smile on his face.

Their curiosity finally getting the better of them, the girls from the pool trotted into the bar, all their courage summoned, giggling furiously, and gingerly approached our table. 'Are you Slash from Guns N' Roses?' squealed one of them, a blonde with blue ocean-wide eyes.

'I am . . .' he answered, belching softly.

'Can I have your autograph?' she squealed again.

'Sure, baby.' Slash put down his glass and cigarette and, rising unsteadily to his feet, patiently signed the proffered bits of paper, T-shirt and skin . . . whatever the girls wanted and wherever they wanted it.

'I love you, Slash,' breathed another who could have been a twin of the first.

'I love you too, baby,' drawled Slash, leering theatrically. The girls clapped their hands and squealed in unison. They left the table walking backwards, waving and blowing kisses.

Slash flopped down in his seat again and looked pleased with himself.

You like all that, I asked?

'Oh, yeah . . . but it's hard for me to go and pick up chicks sometimes, 'cos I resent the fact that I'm getting laid 'cos I'm in a band.'

33

It was clear Slash had little time or respect for the girls that follow bands – the ones that follow bands all the way back to their hotel rooms, anyway.

'Ah . . . I shouldn't really say this but I have a tendency to get really drunk and then I get to the hotel and I'll pick the first chick up that I can get. You'd be surprised at some of the chicks I've picked up. Sometimes you get to the hotel at six in the morning and there's all this . . .' he pursed his lips in disapproval. 'So what you do is you go up to the room and just drink till they look good . . .'

On a serious level, didn't he ever worry about . . .

'AIDS?'

I nodded.

'I knew you were gonna ask that,' he said quietly. 'Yeah, that's a fucked thing – because of the way that I was brought up, or the way that I brought myself up, 'cos it was at a time when I was figuring it out for myself. My whole philosophy was one way and now it's like I've got a stupid thing tugging at me all the time saying, "Slash, you've got to watch out, you're playing with death." It's fucked up because . . . I'm having problems with my girlfriend, right? I split up with her. I can't handle having a girlfriend. I can get laid any time. Except for . . . It's just a fucking drag.'

And using condoms, Slash said, was definitely not the answer. 'I really can't start wearing rubbers. I haven't used one since I was thirteen – and then it split. What can I do? I guess it's just part of the whole thing – if drinking doesn't get me, AIDS will,' he concluded, doomily. AIDS, said Slash, was 'a ghost sent to haunt us. I have this underlying fear all the time. If anything – anything – goes wrong with me then I think, shit, this is it!

'There was a point when we were in London, and I got sick one day. I don't get sick ever, for some reason. But what happened was I hadn't been in London in ages, so I got to the hotel straight from the plane and I just kept drinking and drinking for four or five days. Plus the time difference and all that, that hit me and I got really sick. I was in bed. Then I went out to some pubs with some people and I couldn't drink, I couldn't talk, I couldn't hang out, I had to take a cab back to the hotel. And I was in bed for the next couple of days – this was right before the first gig. I thought, this is it, I'm dying.' He smiled mirthlessly.

'AIDS is just like this constant thing that's on my mind now. Welcome to the eighties, you know? I mean, nobody has said this. I've never heard anyone say this, like, in a magazine. But I think that everyone should realise that as soon as David Lee Roth or Gene

Simmons or me, or any of us goes down with it, then we all go. It's gonna be like clockwork! What rock star do you know of that has died of AIDS? Nobody – yet.' The conversation was getting morbid. 'But as soon as one of us goes then . . . 'cos Dave Roth fucked some chick that I fucked that . . . I think that it's gonna take out a whole legion of people. It's gonna be like, 1989, 1990 – the year all the rock stars died,' he cackled.

Had Slash ever had an AIDS test? And if not, would it be a good idea, did he think?

'No,' he winced. 'But, oh, man, I went out with a porno star for a while . . . I went to a party with the Metallica guys and got so drunk it got to the point where they were carrying me around, and I woke up the next morning in this chick's apartment. It was just after John Rawls, the porno star, died of AIDS. But I was like in hell, and she had a flat tire and no phone. I was stranded with no money and it was just way fucked up. She used to do these things called lodes, which are the equivalent of heroin but they're pills. So she was out of it the whole time and impossible to talk to. My first question to her the next mroning was, "You haven't fucked good old John, have you?" I mean, no, she never fucked him. I found out so it was OK. But at first I was freaking . . .'

More drinks were ordered; Slash switched to beer chasers. Soon Guns N' Roses would be returning to England: in August, to take part in that year's Monsters of Rock festival at Castle Donington. Did it mean anything to Slash still, that he was born in England?

'Oh, yeah, yeah . . . When I was a little kid, they brought me out here to LA with my grandma and I wasn't that fazed by it. Then I went back to England for Christmas. I went back and forth a few times. My earliest memories of America are, like, seeing King Kong on TV for the first time and noticing how it was always sunny . . . The English way is so different. You know, they know how to cook and the food's just different, and everybody's sweet, and it's like you know everybody in that neighbourhood and the neighbourhood doctor and all that.'

I said he made England sound like an old black and white movie and that things certainly weren't like that in my neighbourhood.

'Ah, yeah, but I'm talking about when I was a kid. I didn't live in a big city. So when I first went back to England with the band, I was real happy. Now at this point it's turned into an affection for the rock 'n' roll crowd, because it made a big impression on me the first time I was there.'

What was the new bad boy of rock like as a child, I wondered? Was he good at school, for example?

'I could add and subtract and shit. But when it came to matrix and algebra I was failing miserably at school, and mom tried to stick me in a summer school in an algebra class.

'I'd go in every day and smoke cigarettes. It was just me and the tutor for the first week and a half . . . You know, I do honestly try. So I went and this boring fucking asshole was trying to shove this shit down my throat. I was so sick of it I just split. I wasn't real good at that. But English was one of those subjects that my dad pushed on me at an early age, 'cos he reads and all that. Other than that I was just average . . .'

Did he still have much contact with his family in England?

'I never went back to see my family, 'cos they hadn't seen me since I was a little kid, anyway. Actually I never visit the family,' he confessed. 'So that's sort of deleted at this point.'

How, though, did Slash explain the dizzying success of the band in Britain? From the Marquee, to the Hammersmith Odeon, to a place on the bill at Donington and hit single status in just two quick trips is a feat not many of their ilk had managed to pull off so quickly, or so convincingly. Not Motley Crue, not Bon Jovi, not Poison . . . why Guns N' Roses?

'I really don't know. Right band at the right time, I guess. The first time we played the Marquee, there was such a fucking buzz. I guess the first gig was real sloppy and lax. But then I had a great fucking time. I was hanging out on the street, got drunk. I think I was the most obnoxious I'd ever been when I was in London. I got chucked out of every pub. You know the St Moritz club [in Wardour Street]? I smashed that whole window 'cos they wouldn't let me in! I kicked in the whole window and the cops came and I snuck out of there. I got kicked out of the Limelight club, I got kicked out of the Intrepid Fox.' He sighed, proudly reeling off the names like old war medals. 'All those places in that area I got kicked out of, and I had a great time.

'I fuckin' stole [UFO vocalist] Phil Mogg's drink and poured the glass over my head and threw it back at him in the Intrepid Fox. 'Cos I hate that guy,' he whispered. 'I hate anybody that pulls a rock star trip on me. He came and sat at our table. I just thought he was showing off. I don't know, apparently he's a pretty cool guy. But he sat down and ordered a drink on our tab, I guess, or whatever. The drink came and I took it and smashed the glass. Everybody was, like, shocked. It was so stupid, but I was having such a good time that nothing mattered . . . I was just running around those little streets in Soho yelling – it was a gas! We hung out with Lemmy from Motorhead at their studio. They let us play their gear. Motorhead are like heroes to us, so that was pretty cool.

'London to me is like . . . I want to feel close to that crowd, I want them to feel that we're one of their bands. But we don't play there enough. We've played there twice. We were gonna come back with Metallica, but that doesn't start until October and we'll be off the road by then. Going back and doing Donington is the greatest, though. We've been told they're expecting maybe 100,000 people. That's just like the most important gig . . . Do you know how we're doing it?' he asked, leaning across the table conspiratorially. 'We're doing the Aerosmith tour, I told you, right? Well, we're taking Concorde, playing Donington, then flying back. We're flying back commercial, but we're going business class,' he said with undisguised glee.

'See, Alan our manager is a really good manager, and the cool thing about him is he has a tendency every so often to break down and get indulgent. Like get drunk and suddenly decide to take a limo on to the next place. We need that kind of vibe,' he explained with a straight face. 'Just let's throw all the money into the pot and let's just go!'

Morning turned into afternoon. Outside the sun continued to blaze down on the pool, roasting the inert forms littered around its kidney-shaped curves. We returned to the forthcoming dates in America with Aerosmith. Had Slash met any of the band yet?

'Yeah, I've met the whole band. I went to see them when they played here in LA last time. I got dragged into this room where they were all lined up against this table, signing posters and stuff. I got pushed in front of them and introduced by someone from Geffen. I was like, "Hi . . ." I couldn't think of anything else to say. These guys have been my heroes for life, you know? But I didn't get nervous, I got speechless and it was real weird. They were all looking at me – I had my top hat on, leather jacket and jeans – and there was this vibe like I was being checked out. The only one who actually spoke to me was Steven Tyler. He was like, "How're ya doin'?" and "Where's Axl?" He was real cool. He called us once when we were in Amsterdam. He called us from America and spoke to Axl – to apologise for something he'd said on radio or something like that, which was cool.

'Apparently they're real excited about having us out. I talked to their manager and he said they're looking forward to it because we kick ass and we'll make them kick ass that much harder. So now I'm thinking, I'm gonna have to go out and play my ass off if we're gonna make any kind of mark on this tour.'

Was Slash a particular fan of Joe Perry's guitar playing?

'I've got nothing against Joe, I was into him a little while back. I think the main thing about Joe is he's getting older – basically, he's done it all – yet he's still trying out shit, doing all this new guitar stuff. It's great. But I'm like a die-hard for the old Jeff Beck Les Paul type of stuff.' He smiled. 'Back when Jeff was doing that and when Joe was doing it, too. That's what I'm into. So now I don't really listen to Joe any more, but he still is responsible for a bunch of solos which became like trademarks. I had Aerosmith on the back of my leather jacket – not the new one, that says Guns N' Roses – but I have one back at the hotel that just has a huge Aerosmith on the back. I was gonna wear it on the tour. I'll wear it for a couple of gigs, maybe.'

The members of Aerosmith – notorious hellraisers in their own right back in the seventies – had, of course, since undergone a much-publicised clean-up programme and were now all teetotal, actively anti-drug and quite fanatically health-conscious. Rather limited the opportunity for any 'partying down' between the two bands, didn't it?

'It's a drag,' frowned Slash. 'I mean, I'm glad they're clean and all that but I wish they hadn't got as fucked up as they had, because we're not allowed to hang out with them at all now. This happened to me with Nikki Sixx from Motley. Like, Nikki and me are pretty good friends. But after we did the tour with Motley Crue and Nikki got clean, he grew away from me, I never saw him. Then I ran into him in the Cathouse one night. I was sitting up in the VIP section, just sitting there. And I had four of these tall glasses filled with Jack, and Nikki came by and was sitting next to me. He said, "That Jack smells good." I said, "Oh, do you want one?" Not thinking. He was like, "Oh, no, no . . ." That was so fucked, I shouldn't have done that. So for a while I didn't hang out with Nikki. And it's that kind of thing with Aerosmith, it's very strange. But I respect trying to clean up before you kill yourself.'

Would Slash ever consider anything so dramatic as a complete 'clean-up' himself?

'I don't know what's gonna happen with me,' he yawned. 'I don't know what's gonna happen in the future. Right now I'm just doing what I do . . .'

For how long, though? Wouldn't there come a time for Slash, too, in five or ten years' time, maybe, when he would also have to put a brake on things a little – not just to stay alive even, but to stay sane?

'I don't know if that would happen or not,' he shrugged. 'I don't know how long my system will hold up. I could be superhuman and drink forever, you know what I mean? We are a young band and we've got a real hunger for . . . everything! And that will last as long as it lasts. I know anybody who thinks they're gonna be king of the hill forever has got it wrong. See, I learned that, 'cos of my background with my parents and shit. I've seen everything. I've seen the worst. And I've never met a person who hasn't quit while they're ahead, or it's fucked up their lives.

'The thing about coke and dope and valium and shit like that, you have a great time and it's the best, but eventually it catches up with you. And if it catches up with you and you don't take notice and you get real arrogant about it, it'll . . . you'll be sitting in a rehab centre going to AA meetings every fuckin' day. It's just not worth it to go through all that shit.'

Why start using drugs in the first place, though?

'Well, sometimes it's just curiosity – or 'cos you think you're Keith Richards. We started 'cos we had to try it. But there would be no Guns N' Roses right now if I hadn't stopped and Izzy hadn't stopped.'

Stopped what specifically – one drug in particular or drugs in general?

'Drugs in general but, like, heroin, too. That is one of the things that has fucked up so many people. It really has fucked up a lot of people. So you have to quit. But look at Clapton, he was really lucky, he did some good albums on it. The same with Aerosmith. They all did some great albums. If Keith had a fuckin' buzz he'd probably still be doing it . . .'

Slash grew agitated, restless. The Jack was starting to kick in, perhaps, and the next album was back on his mind. 'I've got to go and do another record,' he said firmly. 'I've got too much shit in my head. It's getting to the point where I'm doing fifteen-minute intros to the songs because there is so much shit happening inside my head, so much shit I want to play. I couldn't bear another six months of "My Michelle". I love the songs and stuff but the new material is so much more . . . a lot of it's meaner definitely – influenced by hanging out with Metallica,' he quipped.

'That whole James Hetfield attitude, I like, though. I spent a wild night with him and Jim Martin from Faith No More, driving out to the Valley just to get drunk. James was in this car throwing beer cans out on the freeway. James always plays at being this manly fuckin' . . . He always reminds me of a Ranger . . . Like, "Goin' out to the mountains." But he's a really sweet guy. Basically, he's not anywhere as mean as he makes himself out. He's just great to hang out with, he's got a great fuckin' attitude. And Lars [Ulrich] is just a sweetheart, too. Those guys are genuinely cool.'

39

Slash obviously spent a lot of time hanging out with musicians from other bands. It seemed a peculiarly insular existence.

He disagreed. 'Actually, there's hardly any bands I can hang out with because there's this constant "I gotta act cool" attitude. LA is the worst. Like that band Junkyard – they're hilarious. Or . . . I went out with the Ratt guys, and Juan [Croucier] is a real sweet guy. But I was talking to Stephen [Pearcy] and it's like, shut the fuck up, just go away, you know?'

Why?

'People like that are always talking about now you've sold a million records you get to do this, you get to do that . . . It's like, I don't give a shit! Great, we sold a million records, I'm really glad we've succeeded. To me it means I don't have to go out and start from scratch again. I hate that "Now you've sold a million records it doesn't matter how good the next one is it'll still sell." I get so sick of hearing it. Like, who cares, just fuckin' play . . .'

And with the millions of records sold came the millions of dollars – or theoretically, at least.

'We just got our first big royalty cheque the other day,' Slash told me. 'It's the first real money we've seen, though it's nowhere near as much as you might think. But now I've got it I don't know what to do with it. Money has never been . . . There was a period after my mom and my dad divorced when she was going out with David Bowie. She was making all his clothes, and I hated it because he took the place of my dad. I was sort of young . . . Anyway, he [Bowie] had a little rented white Mercedes and this huge fuckin' house up in Bel Air that he rented while he was in LA. At that time when I didn't know fuck all about anything. I'd be thinking, what the fuck is this? Why do you have to have a big house? All the to-do he would put into everything was just ridiculous.

'At this point in time I can borrow enough money to take limos everywhere or buy a Jaguar. But it's like, what the fuck for? I don't see any reason to flaunt it because you're successful and you're a so-called rock star.'

Didn't money also buy you an increased sense of security, though – the freedom to cut loose and do whatever you want?

'It doesn't buy you freedom at all,' Slash demurred sourly. 'It brings responsibility, and you have to start making choices you were never asked to make before. Because you've got money now, if you have any brains at all you put it somewhere. If you don't put it somewhere and rock out and spend it all then it's just another obstacle because you're gonna go broke again . . .'

And that's when bands who have hated each other for years suddenly decide it would be a good idea after all to get back together (and make some money).

'Yeah. We'd be back in no time, I tell you!' he laughed. 'Pete Townshend is great . . . I heard him talking on TV one night and he said, "Yeah, we'll probably reform, we need the money." I thought that was pretty funny. I don't know, money is weird. Like, if I went out and bought myself a three-hundred-thousand-dollar solid gold stand to put my TV on – I mean, no one is going to notice but I like it, so fine. But if you buy a three-hundred-thousand-dollar solid gold doormat then that's a different thing . . .'

Slash couldn't make up his mind whether to have one last glass of Jack or not. He was going on to a tattoo parlour on Sunset straight after the interview. He had a design he'd drawn himself – some skulls, a guitar, the obligatory roses and the words 'Drink Til You Drop' scrawled across. Maybe the Jack would deaden the pain, he said. He ordered one, anyway, and thought about it. I asked if he had any other hobbies outside of guitar playing and drinking Jack Daniels?

'Uh . . . I like reading. But the problem with me is I won't take a risk on buying a book that I see just 'cos I like the look of it. I read what people give me. The last batch of books I read were those Anne Rice vampire books. And I read *Islands in the Stream* by Hemingway, which was really boring. Another bad habit of mine is to read books, take it all in and toss them. I read just to read.'

Did he have a favourite author?

'Celine – I read a bunch of his books which were just the best! He's got probably one of the most bitter fucking, most negative outlooks on life I've ever read. It was a great, I read a couple of his books. That was another thing that my dad turned me on to . . . I love reading when it's good, I hate reading when it's crap. That Shaun Hutson guy, a lot of his books are funny. That one about the slugs . . . the part where the couple are squatting – it's fucking great! There's a part when his bum starts getting into a piece of fruit that's been thrown away . . . oh God . . .' he groaned, clutching at his stomach in mock agony.

'I need this shit to go on the road with otherwise I just sit on the bus and go like this.' He slumped his head. 'I am 125 per cent band-oriented. Everything I do is geared to that. When we're on time off I just can't focus on anything else. I used to collect snakes. But I haven't got time to look after the snakes now so I just go out and get drunk all the time and wait for the next gig. We have a manager so there's not much else for me to do. So I don't have any real hobbies. I play my guitar. I don't like to practise but every so often I'll sit down and I'll

41

work on something – I'll write songs. The only time that I really get off is if I write a song and it feels good so I'm playing it. Or being on stage. 'Cos I get really lazy. But on stage, you know, you can just fuckin' wail . . .'

We both said amen to that.

THREE

No Christmas for Drunkies

OCTOBER 1988
In the brief time that elapsed between that first interview with Slash and our next meeting four months later, a lot had happened to Guns N' Roses; enough in fact to transform them from the rising cult stars I had last encountered into a veritable household name, their infamy beginning to settle across entire continents. *Appetite For Destruction* had reached No. 1 in the U.S. album charts in August – exactly 57 weeks after its first entry into the *Billboard* Top 200. And 'Sweet Child o' Mine' matched it by hitting the No. 1 spot in the U.S. singles chart shortly after. The fates appeared to be conspiring in the band's favour again when straight out of left field – on Saturday, August 20, 1988 – tragedy struck.

The place was the eighth annual Monsters of Rock Festival at Castle Donington in the Midlands of England. Guns N' Roses were fifth on the bill; above Helloween and below Megadeth, David Lee Roth, Kiss and headliners Iron Maiden, and the largest crowd in the festival's history – over 90,000 people – was expected to turn up. Donington was, and remains, the largest, most prestigious outdoor event in the British rock calendar, and everybody in the band was looking forward with enormous enthusiasm to returning to England. Axl had *all* his voices back and the band's engine was expected to be revving again after being nicely warmed-up with a fortnight's worth of ecstatically received shows in America with Aerosmith. (The proposed Japanese tour in July had eventually been cancelled in order to give Axl's voice a proper chance to recuperate after his ordeal on the Iron Maiden tour. The Japanese dates would eventually be rescheduled for the end of the year.)

Forty-eight hours before they were to appear on the Donington stage, the band took a short break from their commitments on the Aerosmith tour and, just as Slash had predicted, caught a Concorde flight to London, where they connected with a domestic flight direct to

East Midlands airport. The day of the show began blustery and cold, dark storm clouds looming ominously in the sky – traditional Donington weather, in fact. The first really serious downpour saved itself, with immaculate timing, for the precise moment the opening act, Helloween, took to the stage at 1.00 p.m. sharp. Rain continued to sheet down mercilessly throughout the duration of the hapless German outfit's set, and the fierce wind had blown one of the fifty-foot side-stage video screens from its moorings. Luckily, the screen fell harmlessly onto some empty ground and no one was hurt, but a shudder of foreboding swept visibly through the crowd, at that point in the afternoon still only 50,000 or so strong.

By the time Guns N' Roses arrived on stage at 2.00 p.m. and began trawling out the riff to 'It's So Easy', the rain had temporarily subsided and the sky was a sullen grey. The field the crowd was standing in had turned into a mudbath, however, and at first applause for the band seemed scattered, subdued perhaps by the cold, damp conditions. Then Slash swung a punch at his guitar and the band kicked hard into 'Mr Brownstone', and suddenly the atmosphere started to pick up. Axl cantering from one side of the stage to the other in white leather Guns N' Roses tour jacket, white cowboy boots, waist-tied scarf flapping crazily in the icy breeze, mike-stand held horizontally like a knife, body swaying from side to side just like in all the videos, only much more manic, like a high-speed replay . . .

They followed that with the slowed down semi-acoustic version of 'You're Crazy' that would later appear for the first time on the *GN'R Lies* collection, still some four months away from release at the time of the Donington show. Halfway through the number a disturbance appeared to break out amongst the crowd coiled like a snake around the front of the stage, and the music suddenly ground to a juddering halt. Axl stopped singing and started cursing at the crowd to step back and quit shoving each other. Several bodies appeared to be hoisted out of the mêlée by an assortment of security men and roadies. Confusion reigned as the crowd at the front tried to recompose itself and the band wandered around on stage pointing their fingers and yelling, looking as lost as the rest of us.

After what seemed like an eternity Slash eventually began stroking out the riff to 'Paradise City' and both band and audience attempted somewhat half-heartedly to carry on with the show. But bodies were still being pulled from the crowd and Axl stopped the band mid-song a second time. 'Look!' he yelled, trying to cajole the crowd into calming down, 'I'm taking time out from my playing to do this and that's the only fun I get all day . . .'

The situation appeared to ease again and the Gunners wheeled shakily into 'Welcome to the Jungle'. Black clouds reappeared in the sky above the stage and another torrential downpour threatened. After that the band tried to calm things down further with 'Patience', another new acoustic number receiving its first public airing in the UK and also destined for the *GN'R Lies* mini-album. However, unfamiliarity and the appalling weather conditions bred, if not quite contempt then indifference – at least for the majority of the crowd that didn't have their bodies pressed tight against the security barriers at the front of the stage. The intro to 'Sweet Child o' Mine' received the biggest cheer of the set and was preceded by a little speech from Axl thanking everybody for making it Guns N' Roses' first hit single in Britain. They crunched their way through it with the sensitivity of a mallet then left the stage, clearly relieved to escape their ordeal. There was no encore.

Ironically, Axl's parting words to the Donington crowd that day were: 'Don't kill yourselves!' He did not yet know that two of its members – teenagers by the names of Alan Dick and Landon Siggers – had had the life crushed out of them when the crowd at the front had surged forward as Guns N' Roses took to the stage, causing them to slip and fall. By the time their crumpled, broken bodies had been rescued from the mud and carried to the emergency centre backstage, they were both already dead – Siggers so badly disfigured his friends and family were only able to identify his corpse by the scorpion and tiger tattoos on his arms.

'I saw the whole thing happen,' promoter Maurice Jones later told noted Donington chronicler Jeff Clark Meads in an interview published in *Kerrang!* 'The problems were created by idiots, absolute idiots. They were pushing stage right and the crowd compressed. They just couldn't go any further, then about fifteen feet from the stage, a hole in the crowd opened and people went down. I went down to the front of the stage and I saw First Aid people and the doctors working and I felt so useless . . . I can't describe how it felt. I saw five bodies on the ground and I knew somebody was dead.'

Despite the swift issuing of a statement by Chief Superintendent Dennis Clarke of the West Midlands police division, in which he described the crowd at Donington that year as 'otherwise superb' and announced that there had in fact been no arrests, reaction in Britain's notoriously tacky tabloid press was predictably over the top and the more scurrilous Sunday editions published the following day ran sensationalistic, wholly inaccurate stories claiming, amongst other things, that the stage collapsed and that Guns N' Roses had refused to stop playing even after being informed of the plight of the injured fans.

'We even had very well-known and supposedly responsible newspapers saying the stage had collapsed,' Maurice Jones complained to Jeff Clark Meads. 'The stage didn't collapse and was never in any danger of doing so! The one thing I did learn from all this,' Maurice went on, 'was never trust a reporter. A lot of the press had absolutely no respect whatsoever for the kids who had died and I thought it was completely disgusting . . .'

The coroner's inquest into the deaths returned an open verdict and concluded that there was nothing more that could have been done to guarantee the safety of everybody on the site that day. Indeed, the hearing conceded that it was virtually impossible to absolutely guarantee the individual well-being of every single member of a crowd the size of the one at Donington that year. (Official sources placed the total figure at 97,559, while privately some estimates put the figure at closer to upwards of 110,000 people – though it's worth remembering that less than half that amount had actually arrived by the time Guns N' Roses were on stage.) Even so, straight after the inquest, the local authority, North West Leicestershire District Council, formally placed a crowd limit on all future events at Donington of 70,000, and it would be another two years before the Council would again grant Maurice Jones a licence to hold another festival there.

Meantime, Guns N' Roses were back on the road with Aerosmith in America, and Geffen re-released 'Welcome to the Jungle' as a single to coincide with the September release of the latest Clint Eastwood movie in the *Dirty Harry* series, *The Dead Pool*, which featured the band in a cameo role performing 'Welcome to the Jungle' in a club in Miami. The sequence had been filmed earlier in the year during a break from touring.

By the time I found myself back in Los Angeles in October 1988, the single had already risen to No. 7 in the U.S. charts, and *Appetite For Destruction* was still bobbing like a fly glued to the web of the *Billboard* Top Five. By then the Aerosmith tour had finished and the band were left kicking their heels at home in LA until the re-arranged Japanese and Australian dates began in November.

Slash had called to suggest dinner and drinks and we set off at dusk, the moon rising slowly in the darkening copper-nickel sky, to a Mexican restaurant Slash said he knew of on Sunset where the drinks, he assured me, were served 'strong and without the bullshit trimmings'. Dressed simply in off-white T-shirt, leather jacket and crumpled black jeans, showing three or four days' growth of wiry black bristle on his chin, the dark matted curls cascading down his face even more of a bird's nest than usual, Slash looked drawn, tired; a much older, more haggard version of the smart-talking know-something I remembered from our last encounter just a few months before.

Seated at a table in a corner-booth of the cavernous restaurant, Slash pushed the hair out of his bloodshot eyes and carefully surveyed the scene. 'I know this place is kind of sleazy and rundown but I like it here, I feel comfortable,' he said in his soft only-kidding Californian drawl. 'Me and the band used to rehearse in a garage down the street from here when we first started out, and we used to come here all the time. We always used to sit here in the corner, right where we are now, because it's the best spot to get a blow-job under the table without anybody else in the room knowing,' he mentioned matter-of-factly. 'We used to bring chicks here all the time and get 'em to do that. Or take 'em in the toilets out back.'

'Well, don't think I'm going to stick my head under the table to pay for my dinner,' I told him straight.

'Fuck you, you're too ugly!' he chuckled. 'The food here is so bad you probably wouldn't notice the difference anyway . . .'

A surly crow-faced waiter with blood spots on his white coat and a pencil stub apparently grafted to his lips arrived to take our order. We chose the chicken fajitas and ordered up a pitcher of the house speciality – iced Marguerita. The tequila jug arrived on the table and Slash poured some into a couple of tall salted glasses and we drank greedily. Suddenly the atmosphere of the place, with its dingy red walls and fake gold trimmings, seemed much less oppressive, cheerful even. Slash poured a couple more. While we were waiting for the food I asked him how he was enjoying being off the road for a while.

'Hah . . .' he waved his cigarette dismissively. 'I don't like it, man. I'm bored already, you know?'

But surely, I asked, now was the time to sit back and start reaping some of the rewards of their enormous success over the last eighteen months, wasn't it?

'And do what?' he replied innocently. 'I don't know . . . you're talking about things . . . possessions,' he rolled the word around in his mouth like a pebble. 'I mean, I didn't even have anywhere to live until, like, two weeks ago . . .'

The fajitas arrived with a thud and Slash eyed the dishes cautiously. Then he picked up a spoon and began heaping some of the chicken and sour cream and some of the other mush into a pancake. He rolled it between his fingers and thumbs like an old-style cheroot then forced the squishy end into his mouth. He worked away at it with his jaws slowly for a minute or two, swallowed, then washed what was left down with a slug of the Marguerita. 'Man, these fajitas stink,' he grumbled, still licking his lips. 'I don't know why I brought you here. You must think I don't like you or something . . . You want another drink?'

We pushed our plates away and I asked if we could pick things up where we'd left them four months before – with Slash and the rest of the band flying Concorde, to Donington. So, what was it like, I asked?

'Too small,' he snapped. 'Nice, though. We crossed over fuckin' Texas in about five minutes flat, and on the plane it's almost festive, everyone's like, yeeaaahhhhh . . . here we go! Then they have these, like, high-class meals, right? Which is just expensive microwaved shit – it's the worst! But you get all this food and they treat you very nicely and stuff. And the thing is it was only like a three-hour flight, so we were there in no time. I just drank – to compensate for the shitty food,' he said, reaching for the pitcher of Margueritas.

And what of Donington – how had Slash and the band found the experience as a whole?

'The whole going to England thing was . . . weird.' He shifted uncomfortably in his seat. 'I was put into a situation where I was away from the rest of band, doing things like press and radio. Apart from when we were actually on stage, the only real time I spent at the gig was at soundcheck. The rest of the time I was busy either screwing or doing interviews, so I didn't leave the hotel room . . .' he deadpanned.

What about the incident that sparked the deaths of the two fans: how much did Slash actually see of what took place?

'Well, it got a little bit out of hand and, I don't know, we stopped 'cos we had to stop,' he said, his voice lowered to almost a whisper. 'We just looked out and it was like, oh fuck . . . From where we were standing, which was right above it, it looked really hectic. You couldn't tell what happened exactly but there's a certain amount of force which goes into the first ten rows. You could see that surge when we came on, you could *see* the force. And they're just people . . .' He stared at the food on his plate. 'We stopped because we were scared,' he said, at length. 'Like, let's clear this up. We didn't find out two kids had actually died during our set until we got back to the hotel that night. Alan [Niven] was really bummed out about something and I sort of sat down with him and he told me about it. It just destroyed the whole thing for me . . .'

Did Slash feel in any way personally responsible for the deaths?

He thought about it for a bit then shook his head slowly. 'Not personally, no. The way I see it is – too many people in one place, there's no security, there's no nothing. It's not like doing, say, 80,000 people at Giants Stadium in New York, where there's a line of security at the front and there's a line of security that goes all the way around the entire thing. Donington is just like a stage and a huge field, and 100,000 people is a fuckin' lot of people. When we get back I'll show you the video. We have a new video coming out – it's from Giants Stadium and Donington and you can see the difference.

'Donington's just like, here's the tickets, have a great time . . .' He lit a cigarette and hung his head, still disturbed by the memory. 'What bums me out the most is whoever it was who was standing on top of somebody – you can't stand on somebody and not know they're there! They were so self-involved and selfish that they had to be as close to the stage as possible, and somebody was gonna suffer for it and have to lay under their feet in ten inches of mud. That's what really sucked about it. It was front row security, then a huge fuckin' field – further than we could see – and a bunch of kids who wanted to go out and see a good rock show. The craziest ones are always gonna be the ones in the first fuckin' twenty rows – they're the diehards. But you don't fuckin' have that much disregard for human life that you just have to see a show no matter what the repercussions are or what happens to somebody else during it . . .' He sat there, quietly fuming for a moment.

I asked Slash if the band would ever consider playing Donington again. There was already talk of Guns N' Roses being obvious Donington headliners at some point in the not-too-distant future . . .

'I don't know,' he said hesitantly. 'It was a big fuckin' rush for us to be asked to play it. But we won't be able to do it next year, anyway. If it was the year after, maybe, and it was a good time, I'd like to do it. But if we were headlining I'd change a few things.'

Such as?

'I would change the way the whole thing's run . . . Not the whole thing, but I'd change the way it's set up. You've got to compile areas of people into sections and try to do your best to patrol them. A heavy duty English crowd – that's impossible, I know, but if you're gonna do it you might as well make the attempt at it. There's a lot of money made from that gig and the promoter can afford it, right? 'Cos Donington next time . . . a lot of kids are gonna be scared of going. I mean, the kids that died, chances are they hitch-hiked from some way out place and saved up for a month to go; their parents probably didn't want them to go but they had to go, you know how it is . . . And then they lose their lives in, like, fifteen minutes at some rock festival – which, all in all, is a really insignificant event. And it's their entire existence gone! It just bums me out.

'I've been worrying about whether we should write something to their parents or not. Nothing that comes out of our mouths is gonna sound right, though – some simple rock band they don't even know, that are responsible, as far as they're concerned, for the demise of their children . . .'

I gently moved the conversation on and asked about the Aerosmith tour: had that gone as well as Slash and the rest of the band had expected?

His face brightened. 'It was great, some funny shit happened on that tour. Those guys are all clean now – Joe, especially – and they stay in one central place and do four or five gigs, then move on to another part. But they always have one central base. Even so, they were exposed to us for a lot of the time and they hung out with us.'

Had Slash tried to hide his own drinking from them?

'I tipped it all in a cup,' he admitted with a smile. 'That was still in my walking around with a bottle of Jack stage, so I used to tip it in a cup before we hung out. So it was cool, you know. Although there was one point where Steven Tyler came into my dressing room – I have a dressing room apart from the rest of the guys to do my guitar stuff – and I had one empty bottle of Jack and one half full one in there. Anyway, I left the room for a while and when I came back Steven was in there, looking at tapes and stuff. I said hi, you know. He said, "You drink all that today?" I said, yeah. He just gave me this look and didn't say anything. He started to then stopped . . . that's the way the whole tour was as far as that kinda shit goes.

'Anybody who wanted to go to him for help, though, he was always available. But he didn't push it. Like, Steven [Adler], who was a little bit disillusioned about – just about everything in general. He talked to Tyler about it and he gave him some good advice. In other words, he's been there. They all have. And yet they were so much fun to be with. Oh, we had a ball! We got up and played together here in LA – we did "Mama Kin" together. And they used to stand at the side of the stage and check out our set just about every night . . .'

That must have been odd, I remarked, the first time he looked up and caught Joe Perry watching him from the side of the stage?

'Yeah, it was weird,' he grinned. 'Also 'cos of the similarities – especially, like, me and Joe. Then all of a sudden to look up and see Joe standing there with Steven – it was just . . . *wow*, you know?'

Hadn't Guns N' Roses been intimidated at all, though, by the prospect of opening the show for one of the bands they had, in the past, openly admitted to having partly modelled themselves on?

'We thought about it.' Slash shrugged. 'But the band just decided to really hang on to just being us, regardless of the similarities. So we never had any problems. We never really got too intimidated. I mean, I am a fan. We used to watch them from the soundboard every night. There was a lot of personal stuff happened, too, between the band, which I can't really get into . . . It was just like no other tour that we'd done as far as being close to the people you're touring with.

'The only other band we've been that close to is Motley . . . I used to hang out with Nikki and Tommy. But this was different because it was like, we managed to earn a little bit of their respect just for being a naIf-decent rock 'n' roll band. Just going out there to kick some ass, regardless. That was the one thing that they really appreciated. I was doing one of those slow blues guitar picking things one night and afterwards Steven took me aside and said, "That was amazing!" That really made me feel great. I mean, seriously. That and a couple of other things he did, which I won't mention.'

It was while Guns N' Roses were on tour with Aerosmith that *Appetite For Destruction* had finally gone to No. 1 on the U.S. album charts. Had it come as a surprise or had they been expecting it to happen?

'It was a big surprise! When I talked to you the last time, I wasn't expecting it at all. But it's like, it's just words and numbers, you know?' he said self-effacingly.

Nearly a year and a half on from its release the album was still selling by the truckload – it had recently passed the five million mark in America alone. And even now the band were off the road it was still hanging like a claw to the *Billboard* Top Five. What was it about the album, in Slash's opinion, that provided such huge appeal for people – not just teenagers, either, but kids of all ages?

'I think the only reason it could have possibly gone to No. 1 is that we're filling some kind of gap,' he said, thoughtfully. 'A gap that hasn't been filled by this particular kind of music for however long it's been. That's the only thing I can attribute it to. It's not because the songs are, like, huge hits. They're not, they're just rock 'n' roll songs and fuck the Top Forty, you know? I figure we're just the down and dirty Guns N' Roses band,' he continued. 'Everybody wants to have that album because it's not that safe and it looks good next to the George Michael album . . .'

Indeed, it seemed to me that Guns N' Roses had almost

single-handedly made the concept of 'hard rock' fashionable again.

'Yeah, I know,' he said, wrinkling his nose. 'But I'm not gonna take it to the point where it's gonna have an effect on my personality. I'm not gonna let it turn me into one of those completely insecure rock star types who actually doesn't know the limits of what a fucking pop star means. I deal with it my way, and my way is to treat it very fuckin' vaguely. Like the money . . . I know it's really nice to afford an apartment. I know how many records we've sold, I know all that shit 'cos I'm real business-oriented now. I know what I can and can't do.'

And the fame, the money, had it brought happiness, too, though, the way it was supposed to?

'I'm a basically happy person, anyway,' he sniffed. 'Things still get fucked up and piss me off. But I don't sit around getting depressed about it like a lot of people do. It's like, I could be working at Tower Records again . . . I have nothing to complain about.'

The last time we had spoken, Slash had said the band would be back in the studio 'sometime in October, November', working on the next album. Plainly, that idea had long since been scrapped. But why? Had the sheer scale of their unexpected success triggered a sense of panic, perhaps, over the follow-up? When all was said and done, how did one follow a phenomenon? Many had tried, very few indeed had ever succeeded.

Slash remained nonplussed. 'I'm not going to sit around worrying about how good or how successful the next record is gonna be – I don't fuckin' do that shit. We'll just make the best record we possibly can. As sincere and as *us* as possible. 'Cos I know damn well the reason this album is going where it's going is because we hit a certain fuckin' particular place at a certain time. That's fuckin' great. But I'm not going to walk around with my fuckin' nose in the air. If you think about it, rock 'n' roll bands on the average – with the exception of gigs and albums – are pretty insignificant. You're there, then you're gone and then there's somebody else.'

They say there's only ever one 'first time around' . . .

'Everybody listens to it at the same time and everybody burns out on it at the same time. I mean, like the new Bon Jovi record [*New Jersey*] is great but I don't see the same kind of excitement to this record as I did their last one. I saw it happen to a lot of bands . . . Zeppelin and the Stones, same sort of thing. I mean, the Stones died out real quick – well, they eventually died out to the point where no one was really that excited by them any more. Zeppelin put out shitty records, though, and people were excited by them. It's a weird kind of thing. You can't sit there and try to predict it and analyse it. We'll just go out and do another record.

'My attitude is I'm just a guitar player in a band that's doing real well right now, and I'm gonna have the best time I can have while I'm here . . .' Slash was starting to look bored. He tilted the frosted lips of the pitcher into his glass again and began talking about the new apartment he was then renting. 'It's just this funky little apartment, nothing fancy – furnished. It's got this fuckin' couch and refrigerator and stuff – it's my first real apartment on my own. And if I can afford to have a place of my own then I should have one. I can't live off everybody else forever. I can't just keep being this total fuckin' gypsy.'

But that didn't mean Slash was quite ready for his pipe and slippers just yet. 'The cops have already started comin' by,' he said with a hollow laugh. Slash's new neighbours, it seemed, had objected to the sound of Motorhead being blasted at five in the morning from the apartment of their famous new tenant.

'But I'm settling down,' said Slash. Now it was my turn to laugh. 'No, really. I've got a microwave, and I go to the market and buy those microwave burritos, hot dogs, hamburgers . . . everything. Everything goes in the microwave. Except the vodka – that goes in the freezer. Until Izzy comes round . . . Izzy's classic when he gets drunk,' he grinned, slipping off on a tangent. 'Me, when I get drunk I fall over, I puke, I do whatever is stupid. Izzy is like one of those drunks you see in the movies. He's so entertaining, he's so un-Izzy . . .'

Slash drew another cigarette from the pack. 'So anyway, I got a place, it's cheap. Next I'm gonna buy a house and stuff . . .' He was starting to look bored again. 'So yeah, I'm gonna buy a house . . . I don't think I'm gonna buy a car for a while, though. I'm too psychotic with them. I lost somebody's car the other night,' he said with a straight face. 'I was over at somebody's house and I borrowed their car to get home. But I parked it somewhere and I don't remember where it is. I lost it. It was towed away or something – gone.'

Had he been drunk when he drove the car home?

'Ah . . .' he lit the cigarette. 'It's like, cars, man, I get drunk and I just don't know. I still haven't learned,' he wheezed, smoke pluming from his lips like a chimney.

How, I enquired gingerly, had the writing been progressing for the new album?

His reply was markedly less affirmative than it had been back in June. 'In between all the rest of the shit that goes on every day, I've been writing stuff,' he said. 'I've got an eight track machine at home, so I'm putting it all down on tape. I'm pretty productive.'

I asked Slash to describe a typical day in his present life for me.

'A typical day? Some days I get up at eight-thirty, nine o'clock in the morning. Go down to Geffen – talk on the phone to radio stations. Do all this other shit . . .'

Slash up at eight-thirty in the morning? I raised an eyebrow sceptically.

'Sometimes.' He smiled unconvincingly. 'Depends on how hard I've been at it the night before. I've done phone interviews at five-thirty in the morning – talking to Japanese press and all that shit. Except I don't get up for those, I just *stay* up . . . It's a small price to pay for not having to worry about your rent and getting to work on time,' he added. 'You don't have many responsibilities as a band member – you have to fuckin' be there for the few responsibilities you do have.'

Didn't he secretly enjoy it all as well, though? How often did you see the Motley Crue guitarist, Mick Marrs, or Bon Jovi guitarist, Ritchie Sambora, on the cover of a fan magazine? Whereas Slash was now starting to pick up covers in his own right on magazines all over the world . . .

'Yeah, I do it. I'm up for it. If I don't do it then I'll just sit around and do drugs and get drunk,' he explained sardonically. 'There's also a feeling of if I don't do it no one will.'

Was this a pointed reference to Axl, who had sworn off giving interviews of late?

'Axl's very involved – he does it and gets really into it, then other times he doesn't want to do it. He's very emotional, so I'll do it. But if he wants to he could be talking to fuckin' somebody from *Trouser Press* for three hours . . . Axl does this, this and this – and this, this and this, Axl doesn't do. It's not any particular thing, it's just what his frame of mind is.'

What about the others; didn't Izzy or Steven or Duff like to talk to the press occasionally?

Another slow shake of the mane. 'Izzy doesn't wanna do it. He wants to stay very much in the shadows. Steven doesn't do a lot of stuff because it's never been his role. Duff likes to do stuff, but right now Duff's at a wedding so I do it because this is like twenty-five hours a day for me . . .'

The Marguerita pitcher emptied, Slash switched to ordering triple vodka-and-oranges, and the conversation swung with the inevitability of an axe back to the subject of the next album. When, I asked again, would recording actually begin?

Left: An early shot of the guitarists in the band. From left to right: Izzy Stradlin', Duff McKagan and Slash. (Neil Zlozower) *Below:* W. Axl Rose during his heavily coiffeured phase which first appeared on the video for *Welcome to the Jungle* (Neil Zlozower).

Above, left: Slash after doing our first interview together in June 1988 (Neil Zlozower). *Right:* Drummer, Steven Adler (Neil Zlozower). *Below:* Izzy Stradlin' on rhythm guitar.

Left: Axl onstage during the club days in Hollywood at the Whisky A Go Go. (Neil Zlozower)
Right: Duff on bass. (Neil Zlozower)

Above: Axl onstage. He
always claims that the fact
that his own initials spell
W.A.R. is complete coinci-
dence. (Neil Zlozower)
Right: Slash in typical publicity pose. (Neil Zlozower)

Left: Slash onstage. (Neil Zlozower)
Below: Slash while on the road with Iron Maiden. (Ross Halfin)

Opposite page, top: Castle Donington in 1988. Left to right, Slash, Axl, Lars Ulrich (drummer, Metallica) and Dave Mustayne (lead singer, Megadeth). *Bottom, left and right:* Axl and Slash getting heated onstage. (Neil Zlozower). *This page, left and bottom left:* Axl and Steven Adler onstage at Donington when two members of the audience were trampled to death. *Below, right:* Duff in L.A. (Neil Zlozower). *Overleaf:* Axl at a Hollywood gig. (Neil Zlozower)

'Some time in the New Year,' he replied wearily. 'There's talk of going to Japan and Australia at the end of the year, so there's no point trying to go in the studio right now. Plus, we're pretty burnt out right now. We were on the road for a year and a half ... We'll start rehearsing to go to Japan and I'm sure we'll start jamming then, 'cos we have the place block-booked. So we'll jam a lot, play Japan – which I'm really looking forward to, we're playing the Buddokan, which is pretty legendary. But we'll actually go into pre-production right after we get back from Japan.' Famous last words ...

'I was thinking about spending Christmas in England,' Slash announced suddenly, his thoughts drifting further than the next Guns N' Roses project for a moment. 'I don't know, it depends if it's snowing and all that shit.'

Any particular reason, I asked?

'I don't know ... I still do have family there. I'm thinking of visiting them but they haven't seen me since I was about ten or eleven years old. I don't really know if they're still there. We went through Stoke on our English tour. I could have stopped and gone over there – I knew exactly where it was. I couldn't take the pressure, though. Can you imagine?' he squirmed comically.

I wondered whether the idea he had talked of the last time we met – of going out and doing some outdoor festivals next summer – was now out of the window, with the recording of the album being put back.

'No, I don't think so,' he said. 'But we won't open for anybody any more. The only band that I can think of that we would make a good double bill with is the Stones,' he added prophetically – a fantasy that would become a reality less than twelve months later. Indeed, Slash told me that since the last time we'd spoken he had in fact 'socialised' with various members of the Stones.

'I've met Ron Wood a few times. I met Charlie Watts. Keith I met, and Bill. I've never met Jagger, though. Did you read what Keith said about us in *Rolling Stone*? They asked him, what do you think of Guns N' Roses, and he goes, "Not much."

'He said me and Izzy looked like Jimmy Page and Ron Wood, and he said we were very poseurish. Then they asked him, have you heard the album? And he said no.' Slash frowned, his feelings obviously hurt. 'I, like, I didn't take it personally, though,' he said, refusing to buckle. 'And I don't look like Jimmy Page. I saw him on TV today ...

'I can see where Keith's coming from, though. Having been around some of the greats, like Chuck Berry – it must be hard to see upstarts like us and take it seriously. He needs to hear the record or hang out, I don't know. We're not poseurish ... It's just that we-don't-give-a-fuck rock 'n' roll type of thing.' He continued to mull it over. 'We're just us, trying not to get carried away with being us. We're just the huge fuck-ups that made it big. It's like . . . there's this new movie starring John Hughes, right? In one part he's talking about this guy who is really unsavoury, and he says, "Just tell your mom he listens to Guns N' Roses." It's in the script! It's funny . . . At the same time, it's like, a lot of girls I hung out with, it really screwed them, 'cos we do take things to the hilt. The one cool thing about it is we don't take that shit to the hilt to be bad on purpose. When we party we're probably some of the worst, but then we work really hard, too . . .

'We do have integrity and we're very conscientious about what we do. None of us are dead, and there's a lot of new material and it's like, it's all human. It's just that we have a lot of experiences, just being extreme.'

Nevertheless, I pointed out, the band's reputation had already started to assume mythic proportions. Not a month seemed to go by without a fresh new bit of Guns N' Roses dirt.

'Yeah, I know. "Axl's dead . . ."' he sneered sarcastically.

Or, 'They're all junkies . . .' I suggested.

'Fine, fine,' the voice was impatient suddenly. 'I saw this thing on MTV the other day. They did a ten-minute spot on the fact that I did not kill Axl . . . Axl is not dead! I went, what!? They ran these pictures on the screen: "AXL – NOT DEAD" . . . "JIMI HENDRIX – DEAD". Then a picture of me and the band: "NOT DEAD" then "JIM MORRISON – DEAD". Then they showed a picture of the band again: "NOT DEAD". Then they showed a picture of Elvis – "DEAD?" with a question mark. It was a classic!' he chortled. 'I mean, when it gets to that level, you just can't take it seriously any more.'

I told Slash that in the *Kerrang!* office they had an annual sweepstake at the start of each New Year and laid odds on who out of the rock fraternity were most likely to snuff it in the coming year, and that as far as the *Kerrang!* boys were concerned Guns N' Roses were already odds-on favourites to suffer at least one fatality before 1989 was out.

'I know a lot of people think that,' he said, unfazed. 'But when we really start going over the edge I have a lot of self-control. I don't often fuck-up that hard. Alan will send me out to some ungodly place to clear my head. Or Steven, or whatever. Other than that I don't see anything really happening to us.'

How many times had Alan Niven sent him away?

'Once. I got sent to Hawaii . . .'

To clean up?

'Something like that. But he can't beat me,' he smiled. 'I had a girl fly out.'

He brushed the subject off, as if getting whisked off against one's will for an enforced week of 'relaxation' was something that could happen to anybody. But how long could it go on for? Could Slash imagine what he'd be like at forty?

'No. That's something that's really against my whole beliefs in life. No, I got . . . I'm here now and there's a record to do and by the time we start the next tour I'll be twenty-four. That's as far and as long as I'm gonna look at it. To me it's like, album-tour, cut into sections. We did the first album-tour, now we're doing the next album-tour, and I'll worry about twenty-five with the album-tour after that, you know what I mean?'

Before I could decide an eight-piece Mexican band suddenly struck up a storm in the corner of the room; guitars and trumpets blaring like car horns, voices mewling and keening like cats on heat. Suddenly we had to shout to be heard. Listening back to the tape, it's hard to make out much of what we were saying; for long stretches, as I recall, we just gave in to the Mexican boys and sat there working on our drinks. When the band finally took a cigarette break, Slash started to tell me a story about meeting Zakk Wylde, a young New Jersey guitarist who was then just starting to make a name for himself as the new gun-for-hire in Ozzy Osbourne's band.

'Something happened and we met and kept in touch on the phone – through a girl, a mutual friend, sort of thing,' Slash explained coyly. 'So when he was here in LA with Ozzy I went to see him at his hotel and we hung out for a while. I had one of my surplus bottles of Jack with me and we went up to his room and got fried,' he chuckled. 'We had a good time, we jammed. He plays Les Paul like I do, and he plays sort of like the same kind of stuff that I'm into, but, like, four times as fast . . . He's a good guy, a good guitarist. That's what I like in people – at least in my so-called peers and stuff – is just real people.

'I can't deal with that rock star bullshit, which just permeates this whole fuckin' business. Even in the new bands, who have no business acting like that,' he went on. 'You know, like, "We've got our three chords, 'cos some of the guys in Poison taught 'em to us . . ."' He was getting spiteful again. But at least his sense of humour was returning. 'I just don't care any more, I really don't care. Somebody made a T-shirt for me with POISON SUCKS written on it . . .'

Had he ever worn it on stage?

'No. Axl wore it on stage. 'Cos I'd just gotten it, this was with

Aerosmith, and I was like, shall I wear this? Then I thought, naw, and Axl was like, "I'll wear it!" And off he went. . .'

Wasn't it getting just a little petty, though, all the Poison-baiting? Wouldn't it be better to bury the hatchet once and for all and let the whole thing drop – before it got boring?

'Yeah, but there's never gonna be a relationship there 'cos it's like, even if they come up and say hi and this and that I still have a fuckin' deep hatred for what they're all about.' Slash launched into a long involved story about running into Poison vocalist Bret Michaels one night at the Rainbow in LA. 'Izzy was the one who grabbed him. That was so funny. I was drunk, there was a whole table of us, and I was sitting at the head. The next thing you know Izzy's got Bret Michaels to sit down. So there's Bret in between the two of us . . .'

It didn't take much imagination to see how that might have added a certain nervous edge to the hapless singer's evening.

'Scared shitless,' Slash beamed. 'I was so fucked up and it was like, me and Izzy sitting either side of him, so he's getting it from both ends. In stereo! I mean, I wouldn't like to sit next to a couple of Poison guys like that.

'Another time I had Bobby [Dall] in my apartment,' he grinned wolfishly. 'I was staying at the Franklin Plaza and Steven brought him over. I was in the bedroom dealing with some other shit and Steven had just gone back to his apartment for a second and was coming back, but I didn't know. So I came out into the living room and I looked and Bobby was on the couch. I was, like, what is this fucking guy doing in my apartment?'

I said I imagined Bobby was pretty startled himself.

'He was tripping over himself just trying to make amends. That's when I first decided, OK, fine, we'll leave it. Then they came out with their next video and it's awful!' he cried. 'It's an insult to my intelligence for them to do what they're doing. What we're doing has nothing to do with that.' He scowled. 'Like, I can say hi and hello, I don't have anything against them as people. I just hate what they play. I guess there's a place for it and it works . . .' But – the message was clear – not for Slash.

Perversely, it occurred to me that Guns N' Roses may even have owed their popularity, in some measure, to the fact that bands like Poison did exist. Wasn't that, after all, what made the whole concept of Guns N' Roses so thrilling, so unexpected – the band that really didn't give a fuck?

'Like I said, we filled a void which someone had left a long time ago. Aerosmith used to do, I think, what we do. But even Aerosmith isn't the same thing any more,' said Slash, careful not to commit himself too much. 'Even though they're still around, because they're older and experienced, been through the mill and this and that, they're on another plateau now where they're not gonna fill that gap that they left. So along come these guys . . . us, right? And we're, like, fuckin' . . . just going for it.' He waved the waiter over for one last triple vodka-and-orange.

Could Slash imagine the day, though, when he would walk into the support band's dressing room on a Guns N' Roses tour and might see the young guitarist swigging from a bottle of Jack Daniels, and actually say to him: "Wait. You don't know what you're doing . . ."?

'I don't know, you never know,' he replied vaguely. He looked restless again, tired, ill, bored. 'I wouldn't do that, though, because I've never listened to anybody. That was the cool thing about the tour with Aerosmith, 'cos they know that mentality . . . Like, fuck you when you start to preach to me! It just goes in one ear and out the other. It doesn't even make it through one ear. Aerosmith were aware of us and what we were like, but they didn't feel they had to tell us all about it. The cool thing is the guys in our band are aware of it too. I know where my access is. I know where they're gonna take me if I don't at some point . . .' he trailed off ominously.

'You just gotta keep the shit in check. I've been drinking a lot for a long time and I'm only twenty-three years old, and I know that, right? It's not something that I'm just so ignorant about that I'm going on this major blow out, until all of a sudden something stops me physically. I'm more aware than that, but I'll do it anyway,' he insisted. 'So if anything does happen, I won't be complaining about it, 'cos I knew, you know? I *knew* . . . But I have a great time so, to me, my whole philosophy is, like, go out there and fuckin' rage. If I can't, who can?'

He had a point there. You had to hand it to him. Millions already did . . .

Some weeks after this interview took place, Geffen Records issued their first 'new' Guns N' Roses product for eighteen months: an eight-track collection, half live, half studio out-takes which they marketed as a mini-album, designed in the absence of any new material to meet the demand for more Guns N' Roses product.

It was originally slated for release on 11 October but eventually appeared worldwide on 5 December 1988. The original title was *Guns N' Roses: Lies! The Sex, The Drugs, The Violence, The Shocking Truth!* but this was shortened to the more dealer-friendly *GN'R Lies*.

Side one featured the original four tracks from the 1986 *Live ?!*@ Like A Suicide* EP; while side two included four of the tracks from their acoustic sessions with producer Mike Clink in Los Angeles almost a year before: 'Patience', 'Used to Love Her', 'You're Crazy' and 'One in a Million'.

For their devoted fans, however, *GN'R Lies* was as new as things were going to get for some time to come and they cherished it in their millions. Which is exactly what the chief execs at Geffen had in mind when they first conceived of the idea – only no one could have predicted the extent to which the 'new' Guns N' Roses 'mini-album' would take off, selling more than five million copies in America and going on to become a Top Ten hit all over the world over the coming months. And why not? After all, very few of the 1988 buyers of *Appetite For Destruction* had access to the original limited-edition Uzi Suicide release of *Live ?!*@ Like A Suicide*. (Secondhand copies of the original EP had in fact been changing hands for up to a $100 a throw.)

The design and layout of the sleeve for *GN'R Lies* deliberately parodied that of the British tabloid newspapers that had so unfairly castigated them after the shoddy debacle of Donington. 'It's supposed to be like the *Sunday Sport* meets the *Sun* kinda thing, you know, with a Page Three girl on it and stuff,' Slash tried to describe it for me.

Beginning with the familiar hair-raising cry of a crazed and anonymous MC, 'HEY FUCKERS! SUCK ON GUNS N' FUCKIN' ROSES!!' Steven kick-starting the band into the brutal faster-than-the-speed-of-night riff to 'Reckless Life', Axl leering like a jester, 'It's my only vice!' then scurrying like a rat through Rose Tattoo's cheesy hymn to the depraved and the dispossessed, 'Nice Boys (Don't Play Rock 'n' Roll)', followed by their own early autobiographical stab at much the same thing in 'Move to the City', and ending, of course, with the best version of 'Mama Kin' Aerosmith never recorded, side one of *GN'R Lies* at least served to demonstrate to the millions of fans around the world that still hadn't had a chance to see the band play live yet what a raw, lurid entity Guns N' Roses actually were in the flesh, right from the very beginning.

For longer-serving Guns N' Roses aficionados, however, the acoustic set on side two was where the real interest lay. Opening with the unmistakable sound of Duff's voice lazily counting in the beat, 'Patience' was the first song Guns N' Roses had ever recorded that didn't have razor-edged electric guitars and bludgeoning two-fisted drums all over it. In fact there were no drums at all, or electric guitars. Instead there was just the sound of Izzy, who wrote the song, and

Slash and Duff on three sweet acoustic guitars, Axl whistling the melody like a moonage Fred Astaire strolling beneath an artificial sky, the collar of his coat turned up, cigarette in hand, before stooping before the mike to croon like a sheep-killing dog.

'We did this EP for the same reason as we did the first live EP,' Slash explained. 'It's material that we wanted to get off our chests but without taking up too much space. And it's real simple, real sloppy. You can hear us talking, there's guitar picks dropping. Real off-the-cuff stuff . . .'

'Used to Love Her' followed: a slice of misogynistic humour worthy of Lou Reed's Velvet Underground era or the Rolling Stones' 'Dead Flowers' period in its enviable ability to make one laugh out loud. As Axl wrote on the liner notes: '"Used to Love Her" is a joke, nothing more. Actually, it's pretty self-explanatory if you ask me!'

'I think it's pretty fuckin' funny,' said Slash. 'I don't know anybody who hears it and doesn't find it funny, except for the people that never find jokes funny . . .'

'You're Crazy', however, was definitely not a joke. Slowed down from the amped-up methedrine-fuelled version on *Appetite For Destruction* the guitars – both acoustic and electric – belly-crawl like snakes through the quicksand of Axl's claustrophobic search for love.

'It's a lot bluesier, which is the way me and Axl and Izzy originally wrote it. I think I prefer the slower version, it's got something,' said Slash. 'And . . . I don't know, but every time we do "You're Crazy" in that slower style something weird happens, something magical. We've never done it the same way twice . . .'

However, it was the final track, 'One in a Million', which would truly deliver the storm of protest and controversy promised by the album's psuedo-provocative sleeve. Originally titled 'Police and Niggers' and set in the same hazardous time and territory in Axl's life that had inspired earlier, if less downright savage, precursors such as 'Move to the City' or 'Welcome to the Jungle' – poor urban white boy from the sticks arrives in the big bad city of his dreams only to discover the streets really are paved in slime – 'One in a Million' took that premise to its bug-eyed and snarling apotheosis.

At the time of speaking to Slash in the El Compadre, however, I hadn't heard any of the new songs on *GN'R Lies*, and so Slash and I agreed to can any further serious discussion on the subject until I had a chance to listen and make up my own mind.

The cheque for the mostly untouched meal came and we left the restaurant and walked out into the cold refreshing night air of West Hollywood, the neon of the Strip easily outshining the stars in the sky.

We climbed into the car and Slash, who I hadn't seen anywhere near a Jack Daniels bottle all evening – unusual for those times – explained out of the blue that he had in fact called a temporary halt on his Jack-swigging ways, in favour of the warm inner glow of neat vodka, kinder on the breath (and kidneys). Stolichnaya was best, he said.

'It's just that my tongue got black stripes on it. It's a mix of the tobacco in cigarettes and the Jack, which has charcoal in it. That's what was making these black stripes on my tongue. The first time I noticed it I was like, what the fuck! My teeth were really getting stained, too. Then I started drinking it with Coke, thinking that would help, but that didn't work either. Then eventually I thought, fuck it, and Duff talked me into switching to vodka. Duff always drinks vodka. So then I started drinking vodka and my tongue returned to a normal colour and my teeth are clean again.'

The moral being, if you want to keep your teeth looking Colgate bright . . . drink plenty of vodka?

'Uh huh,' Slash grunted, punching the cigarette lighter on the dash. 'And don't drink Jack for five years straight. A bottle a day for five years, that's what I was doing.' He looked puzzled by the thought for a moment. 'Plus, you have really bad breath in the morning – you know, you can't have sex in the morning till you've brushed your teeth, which is a real fuckin' drag,' he mumbled, his eyelids drooping.

The car started and we moved off.

FOUR

High in the Hills after Dark

MARCH 1989

It was round midnight when the fucker finally called. I had just spent my third successive evening holed-up at the apartment of a friend in West Hollywood, waiting for word to filter down from the hills that Slash was finally 'ready' and 'able' to sit down and talk to me. Originally, our taped rap had been scheduled to take place forty-eight hours before. At 1.00 a.m., to be precise, when Slash got off rehearsal. That is, as far as anything ever could be 'scheduled' with the increasingly errant guitarist.

'Right now, he's into staying up for three days straight, then crashing out for the next two,' I was reliably informed by a mutual acquaintance. 'It all depends what cycle you catch him in,' he had added, with a nervous laugh.

And so I had waited. I didn't dare leave the apartment in case Slash chose just that moment to call, and so I sat it out in front of the TV, nibbling takeaway pizza and imbibing cheap supermarket beer. After another slow evening falling asleep at the wheel in front of the game-shows and soaps, I was ready to give it until midnight before I called the whole thing off and booked myself a seat on the next available flight back to London. After all, what the hell was I supposed to talk to him about this time, anyway? I pictured the scene . . .

'Hi, how's it going?'

'OK.'

'Sold many records lately?'

'Yeah. Millions.'

'Made a new album yet?'

'Well, no . . .'

'Going to soon?'

'Maybe.'

'OK . . .'

'Yeah . . .'

63

'Well, see you around!'

'Yeah, see ya . . .'

But with Guns N' Roses having recently made history as the first act for fifteen years to have two albums – *Appetite For Destruction* and *GN'R Lies* – nestling in the *Billboard* Top Five simultaneously, and a new single, 'Paradise City', already shooting like an arrow into the bleeding heart of the American Top Ten, the world's rockzines were in a feeding frenzy for more hot Guns N' Roses copy, and who was I to argue? All the same, it was Friday night in LA – party hearty capital of the known planet – and what was I doing? Watching *Dynasty*. I had called Slash's number during the first commercial break and been told by Adam, his guitar tech, that his young master was still sleeping. 'So what does that mean?' I asked wearily. 'Am I wasting my time here?'

'It means he could sleep right through till tomorrow night, or he might wake up at any time,' said Adam, doing his best to be helpful, even if what he had to say wasn't. 'What do you wanna do, man?'

I ripped opened another can of beer and thought about it . . .

When the phone rang just after midnight, I was in the bathroom, staring at the mirror, still chewing it over. The sound of the guitarist's slurred voice telling me to come right over snapped me out of my reverie. Two minutes later I was out on the road, merging with the late-night traffic on Sunset, headed like a slow-moving crab for the steep brown Hollywood hills twinkling in the gloom beyond the neon-encrusted skyline to the north.

Slash had moved from the small apartment he was living in the last time we met, and was now renting a large house at the top of a narrow dirt road wound high into the very heart of the hills. With only enough room to support one vehicle at a time, and a sheer drop of several hundred feet down one side of the road, it couldn't have been a comfortable drive to make at any time of the day, let alone in the dead of night. The view, though, was something else . . . all of Toy Town splayed out beneath me like a dark coat of stars. I was just anxious I was about to become a part of that view . . .

'Cab drivers refuse to take me here,' Slash told me later, a genuinely puzzled expression on his face. 'The last part of the road is so bad it makes it easy for your tires to skid, I guess. We had a limo nearly go over the side the other night . . . It doesn't seem to stop people just comin' by whenever they feel like it, though,' he added ruefully.

The front door of the house led directly into a spacious living area, which had half a dozen miniature red Marshall amps stacked against one wall, about the same amount of guitars both in and out of their cases scattered around the room, and, curled up in a ventilated glass case in one corner, one of three snakes Slash had recently purchased – Pandora, an eight-foot python with, Slash assured me, 'a heart of gold'. Another python and a boa constrictor were being looked after by friends, he said, until he moved into the new house he had finally bought himself, which was then still in the process of being decorated and made ready for the arrival of its exotic new owner.

For the time being, however, this was home for Slash: *King Kong* flickered silently on the TV screen; on a shelf beside the TV there was a stack of video cassettes, including *A Clockwork Orange, Richard Prior Live in Concert, Aerosmith in Concert, Scarface* and *Animal House*. With the exception of the books that came with the lease of the house – mostly medical encyclopaedias, oddly, as far as I could make out, and geographical directories – the only books in evidence that Slash actually claimed to have read were a well-pawed copy of *Separated at Birth* and an unofficial biography of Frank Sinatra.

I followed Slash into the kitchen and deposited the beers I had brought with me in the refrigerator while he fixed us both a Jack and Coke. 'I got bored with the vodka,' he explained over his shoulder as I eyed the family-size bottle he was peeling the cellophane from. 'Is this breakfast for you?' I asked as we settled ourselves down in a couple of armchairs next to the snake case.

'Uh ... I'm not sure.' He smiled weakly. 'It's either an early breakfast or an incredibly late lunch, I can't make up my mind . . .'

Shoeless, dressed in a black Misfits T-shirt, black jeans and white socks, Slash looked like a man who hadn't woken up properly yet; like he'd much rather believe he was still asleep in bed and this really was all just a dream. He looked impossibly tired, all played out, done in. And though he did his best to conceal it, it was apparent immediately that Slash's nerves were jangled. He was jumpy as a cat. Why, I could only speculate. Was it just the sleepless nights catching up? By his own admission, I knew his coke intake had risen considerably in order to give fuel to those sleepless nights. But that was nothing new: Slash liked to binge periodically, everybody knew that. And so far, he'd always come out of those binges unscathed, untouched, the wisest, tightest ass in the room. Now there seemed to be something else eating into him. I would try to coax it out of him, but he only allowed the conversation to circle in those directions a couple of times. It was 'everything and nothing', he said, burying it before I had a chance to even brush away the earth from the casket.

The phone, typically, never stopped ringing and more than once whatever Slash was hearing on the other end of the line threatened to scupper the whole interview. Nevertheless, after all the waiting around and the on-off-on-again phone calls in the middle of the night – all begun weeks before my arrival back in LA – it was, in spite of everything (or maybe just because of everything), a good time to catch the thoughts of the kid who played lead guitar in what was then, after all, the most sought-after rock 'n' roll band in the world – not to mention the most dangerous . . .

When last we'd met, Slash had spent a good deal of the time complaining about how difficult it was adjusting to being off the road again after eighteen months of solid touring. Since then, he'd had another five months to get used to it, but he still wasn't entirely comfortable with the situation, he said.

'The thing about being on the road constantly is that you never really have any big problems hanging over you. When you're moving around from place to place the whole time you don't think about anything except getting to the next gig. Then when you come off the road, it's like this whole other world that you thought you'd left behind, but that's been waiting for you to come back to it so it can start fuckin' with you again. I mean, I hate having to deal with normal day-to-day shit. It leaves no time for anything else . . .' He got up and slotted a cassette into the tape-deck and soon the familiar, raucous sounds of the Sex Pistols, Rose Tattoo, Motorhead and others filled the room with their own peculiar brand of background static.

How long had Slash rented this place for?

'A couple months, till I get into my own place. What happened was, when I had the apartment I was in last time I saw you, it got so hectic and crazy that I ended up having to sort of sneak out of it. You know, I had the cops there every day and there was a lot of heavy traffic,' he said, in a voice as thick and slow as oil. 'It was just a bad scene after a while – everybody knew where it was. So I snuck out of there and spent a little bit of time sleeping on people's couches again. Finally my broker found me a house to lease until I could get into the place I've bought. But I got really sick and when I came up here to get the keys I was so sick I didn't have the patience to deal with it. So I left and went back to somebody else's house and slept on their couch for a few days, then stayed at somebody else's place. So I had the house for two weeks before I even slept in it.

'Not all this shit's mine,' he added, waving an arm heavy with bracelets in the direction of the bookcases and furniture. 'The Marshalls, the stereo, the magazines, the TV set and the guitar – that's all that's mine, that I care about. So I've only spent about a week sleeping here. I couldn't adjust to it at all at first . . .' the words disappeared into another oilslick as the phone by his side rang for the first time. Slash was either badly out of it or he was sleep-walking his way through this one. Both, probably. But, he said, he 'wanted to get some shit down'. And so we did . . .

He hung up the phone and I asked if he lived in this big house all on his own.

'No, downstairs there is Adam, my guitar tech. I have to leave here in about a week or so, anyway.' He passed a hand across his forehead, mopping at a thin sheet of sweat that had gathered there. He wiped his hand on his jeans. 'Then I'm back out trying to find myself a place to stay, because my house is being decorated and painted and this and that. So it's gonna be about a month and a half before it's actually livable. I don't have the patience to live there while people are coming in and out all day long and all that shit. I've been trying to figure out where I'm gonna stay. I'm gonna stay at Alan's house, maybe. Or Steven's house . . .'

What were the band 'officially' supposed to be doing at the moment, I asked hopefully – already anticipating the answer.

'Writing and rehearsing,' he said without a trace of irony. The eyes remained expressionless. 'Supposed to be, anyway. There's a lot of songs I've written that Axl's really excited about. I have to teach them to the rest of the guys in the band. That's basically what I'm supposed to be doing now. But I've missed rehearsals with them. They've missed rehearsals with me . . . Izzy's got a few songs. I had him over for a few days and we managed to get them onto tape. Then in a couple of weeks Axl's gonna come down and start putting melodies and lyrics to this stuff. Hopefully, we'll be in full-blooded pre-production in about a month and a half . . .'

I reminded Slash that that was what he'd said last time.

He sighed wearily and padded off to the bedroom to find his cigarette lighter. The phone rang and he took the call from there. When he came back, ciggy torched, he asked: 'Where were we?'

I tried putting it another way: had it taken this long to write the songs for the first album?

'The whole thing now is completely different. A lot of the songs on *Appetite* were written over a space of time. There was no kind of deadline or anything. But there was a couple of the songs which were written right during pre-production for the album – like "Mr Brownstone" and "Sweet Child". So we had all the various song-writing scenarios on the first album. But I don't think this is gonna be too far off – writing all the songs and then going in and doing it. It's just getting us all in the same room at the same time that's the hard part . . .'

67

At one point, Slash said, the band had even discussed moving into one big house together and trying to write that way. 'Axl was keen on the idea, but I was . . . hmmm. But I got to the point where I was very seriously thinking about it – because the situation that we're in now, we tend to get too distant. So, I was getting to the point where I was going to live at Izzy's house, or maybe with Duff or Axl, or something like that. The main thing was, Axl and I were going to get a house together – if it was big enough, right?' he added, acknowledging the obvious naïvety of the plan with an indulgent smile.

It would have to be a pretty big house to hold the pair of you comfortably, I remarked.

He kept smiling but he didn't take the bait. 'I went and looked at this house with him, but it was too posh and ritzy for me. Anyway, so now we're all basically living in the same area, so that's good enough. And we have the studio block-booked twenty-four hours a day, so we can hang out there and stuff . . .' Another echo from our previous meeting. The phone rang again.

I sat there and considered. All this talk of twenty-four-hour block bookings and an allegedly increasing stack of 'bitchin'' new tunes, yet the band seemed to be spending less and less time actually together 'in the same room at the same time'. Why? When they had nothing, they at least had each other. Now, with the world at their cowboy boots, I wondered if the success – and with it the means to be entirely self-sufficient (if not necessarily the ways; you can't buy those, you have to learn them) – had conspired to drive Guns N' Roses further apart than was perhaps good for them at this stage of the game, at least for the purpose of writing and recording together?

'No, actually,' Slash insisted, the phone temporarily back in its cradle. 'Because the success had fucked with everybody's heads so much, we're, like, clinging to each other for support, just to keep some sort of mental balance. I mean, I was thinking about it the other day. The success has basically just exaggerated everybody's personalities . . .'

If that was the case, which aspects of his personality did Slash think had been exaggerated the most?

'Erm . . . for me, it's sort of like being anti-social, I guess. Basically, whatever everyone's described me as, it's just made me worse.'

Was he over the sheer rush of having a No. 1 single and album first time out?

He paused again, eyes slitted as though listening to a voice down deep inside. 'Erm . . . actually, it hasn't really been a real high. The initial high was doing those first few tours, that was the best of it. Being off the road and realising you're as successful as you are doesn't really make you feel . . . at least it doesn't make me feel all that excited. Because to me it's like, well, we're off the road and now we have a lot of money, and we can do whatever we want. Except there's nothing that I want to do but fuckin' play. I just want to get back on the road. I envy all the guys who have their new albums done and they're ready to go out,' he added, wistfully. 'I'd love to have the album finished already . . . We spent eighteen months on the road, and it's been a real trying mental thing trying to get back to what other people would consider normal.'

Slash went on to bemoan the fact that he couldn't move around as freely in public as he used to. 'Because the band are sort of like cartoon characters now, you know, people come up to me and it's like, "Hey, dude, drink this beer . . . do something crazy!" They're constantly trying to grab at you, you know, sit down with you and be your best buddy for five seconds. It's just really awkward. I find that going out to clubs – which is something I used to do every single night and get trashed – isn't something I can really do and enjoy any more.

'It's actually at the point where I go to a club and end up leaving totally depressed. It really brings me down. Everybody wants to have your undivided attention, and if you don't give it then they act like you're an asshole – turned into this big rock star now, you know . . . It's something everybody goes through, though, I think.' He shook his head balefully. 'You just can't do it, you know? And it's like, they never wanted my attention before . . . It's really a pretty traumatic experience.'

So how did Slash deal with it then: what was the answer?

'I just don't really go out,' he said flatly. 'There has been a real downside to all this. I don't go out much, I don't have that many close friends, and the few close friends I do have, the times I actually see 'em are few and far between. It gets to be a little bit lonely after a while . . .' The phone rang again.

For someone claiming to be lonely and short of friends, I commented when he'd finished the call, he'd certainly given his new phone number to a lot of people.

'Yeah, but those aren't friends, they're just people who got the number from somebody who got the number from somebody else, you know?' He gave a huge sigh as the phone rang again. This time Slash ignored it and padded off to the kitchen to refill our glasses.

When he returned, I asked about a girlfriend: was he seeing anyone regularly at the moment?

'Ah . . . not really, no,' he stuck his nose into the glass of Jack and inhaled deeply. 'The situation with women, of course, that's all fucked up, too. The girls you tend to run into – the ones that are only interested in you 'cos you're in a band – they tend to be pretty . . . erm . . . pretty low, I think. I don't know.'

Was a relationship something Slash would like to have in his life right now?

'I'd like to have one with the right person,' he said quietly. 'Somebody who had their own career and had their own life. My old girlfriend ended up being so dependent on me, I couldn't take it. It got to the point where her dependency on me sort of drove me out. Then when we split up I realised that everybody else is sort of . . . I don't know, you need to find someone really special and it's just not that easy. Basically, in the kind of places I would be known to frequent, the kind of girls there are just more of the same. It's depressing. There's just a bleak kind of aura around them . . .'

As indeed there appeared to be gathering around this whole conversation. I had never seen the young guitarist so downcast, and worse, so tinged with bitterness. But why? What did Slash really have to be so bitter about?

'I don't know.' He looked away. 'It's a weird feeling. It does fuel the fire for some pretty emotional material, though,' he said, trying to inject something positive into the conversation. 'It's like, the songs we wrote when we were nobody and being fucked with all the time and hassled and we were the outsiders and the underdogs – those experiences provided us with all the material we needed for the first album. And the first album wasn't all that bitter. Some of Axl's lyrics are fuckin' hilarious.' He plucked a smile out of nowhere. 'Now, though, it's like, the amount of bullshit that we have to put up with and the amount of crap we have to take from people has changed. It's more to do with the fact that you can't just find people to be close with and maintain any normal sort of lifestyle. It just starts to make you very bitter, and then you start to write about things in that vein. So it's not like there's a lack of material. It just sort of shifted from one fucked thing to another . . .'

In the days – seemingly aeons ago now – when Guns N' Roses were making their first hard-bitten recordings, they must have wondered what it would actually be like to make it so big. Now that they were, how did the reality compare with the dream? 'I don't know, 'cos I never used to think about it. For me, anyway, it's always been the complete opposite. Fame and what might or might not happen in the future was never part of the trip for me. I've always focused on now, the present. I never try to suss things like that out or try to plan them. But everybody in the band has different personalities and they would all answer that question differently. That's just how it was for me in the beginning, when we first started playing.

'The only times I've kind of come face to face with how the outside world sees us is when . . . Like, I was sitting at home one night, in my old apartment a few weeks back, watching an Aerosmith video. It was from the Cow Palace in 1975, or whatever, and it was like I was fourteen or fifteen years old again – just totally getting into it, you know? Then it dawned on me that that's where we are at this point. That's it! It was just like a total mind blow!' Slash looked sincerely animated for the first and only time of the night. 'Unless you walk around seeing yourself as some fucking rock star all the time, then you're just another humble guitar player, the same humble musician that you always were – who happened to be fortunate enough to be successful,' he said, reaching for his glass.

'Basically, having achieved success and done it without selling out to anybody, though, it's kind of pointless to complain about the other little things. Thank God we've gotten what we've gotten, you know? So I don't like to sound like a prissy little brat going, "Oh, I can't go out any more!" he feigned a hysterical wingey voice. 'But, I mean, it does affect you in an emotional way. When you sit around and think about it too much you can get a little bummed out.'

The phone rang again and this time Slash answered it, then made a face to indicate he wished he hadn't.

Apart from the seemingly endless rounds of 'writing and rehearsing', Guns N' Roses had also set aside time recently to shoot some new video footage, some of which I'd heard was to be edited down into a promotional clip of them doing 'It's So Easy'. Why would the band want to do a video now for a single that was first released almost two years ago? Were they planning on re-releasing it?

'Yeah, maybe,' Slash said, but he seemed vague on the point. 'We always wanted to do a video for that song. It's got that sort of punk attitude to it – especially since Duff was majorly into that, you know, being a former punk rocker and all. And we just wanted to . . . Well, we're gonna have a home video at some point, so we wanted to do some videos that were, like, completely no holds barred, uncensored type of things. Just live shooting, instead of worrying about whether MTV is gonna play it. Just go out there and do a fuckin' blown out live, real risky video . . .'

Guns N' Roses were so hot by then, I said, MTV would probably show it anyway and just bleep out the fucks . . .

'I don't know, I've no idea. I don't really give a shit, to tell you the truth,' he said, glaring at the phone, almost daring it to ring.

Video-making, in general, however, didn't seem to be a process Slash had a lot of time for.

'It depends . . . We've done three videos already – four now, with the new one we've just done for "Patience". That was OK. Easy enough . . . I just sat in this bed playing with my snakes. It was kind of cool. There's something about all our videos I like. I just don't like the boring side of actually making them. I'd always rather be doing something else . . . The video for "It's So Easy" should be cool, though,' he continued in a voice like pennies rolling across a polished floor. 'It's not finished yet, though, we're just going through the final edits. We're supposed to see it Tuesday. It's more or less just for us, so we're gonna tend to put the harsher stuff in and then leave it like that. I don't care whether MTV plays it or not,' he repeated. 'Plus, I want some special stuff on the home video anyway, that's just ours and that you can't get anywhere else.'

What else did they have planned for the home video, I asked? Would it include any of the rough footage shot of their gigs in the days when they were about to sign with Geffen? (I had been shown some once and it was quite breathtaking; the band ravishingly raw, baroque almost, Slash lurching violently across the stage like a disjointed marionette with its strings all cut.)

'Erm . . . I really haven't got a clue at this point. I want . . . I mean, the next album's got to come out first before we even start to focus on that.'

Here we go again then, I thought. So when will the . . .?

Slash shook his head once more and began to say the same words over again that I'd already heard twice before . . . how the band was still writing, still rehearsing, still recovering from the exertions of the last tour . . . only this time he wasn't smiling as he said it. 'We're not adhering to any kind of plan at all,' he explained, in case I wasn't getting the picture. 'There are no deadlines or anything any more. So that being the case, the way we're writing now . . . it's the beginning of March, right? April, May, June, July . . . Maybe June or July.'

Maybe June or July what? Starting the album or finishing it, I prodded.

'Oh . . . starting,' he replied earnestly.

So there was, in fact, little chance, then, of there being a new Guns N' Roses album before 1989 was out?

He nodded solemnly. 'But then that's all in a purple glow. We shall see . . . he said, putting his foot firmly in his mouth,' he kidded. The phone rang . . .

I told Slash that a new rumour had been doing the rounds in LA; that the band were abandoning the idea of making one whole album and were instead considering putting out a series of EPS – each in a different style: rock, rap, acoustic, electric . . . Was there any truth in it, I wondered?

'We were talking about doing an EP of cover songs,' he confessed. 'I don't know . . . B-sides and stuff like that. It's just that there's a lot of stuff we want to record. So we've been flipping through ideas, yeah.'

Almost unbelievably, the phone rang again. 'This is the last call, I'm taking the fuckin' thing off the hook after this!' Slash growled, snatching at the receiver.

It was Izzy on the line. He had some 'friends' he wanted to know if he could bring by. I checked my watch. It was nearly 2.00 a.m.

Slash slammed down the phone, his patience gone. 'They want to come to my house for some after hours drinking,' he grumbled. 'That's always the way it is. They go to the clubs until two in the morning and then it's always, "Let's go see Slash. Slash is always still up . . ."'

So, I enquired gently, you told them no, they couldn't come over? He lit a cigarette and angry white clouds of smoke fumed from his nostrils. 'No, I told 'em it was OK. I don't like saying no . . . Shit, what can I do?' he said, studying his toes. 'They'd only come over anyway . . .'

We got back to discussing the idea of a Guns N' Roses EP of cover versions. Which songs would they choose?

'There's lots we'd like to do, it's which *ones* we're still trying to figure out. We were talking about doing "Jumpin' Jack Flash", and a Steve Jones song that he wrote and sang in the Sex Pistols called "Black Leather". And a Misfits song too, maybe. Just a couple of different things, I don't really like to get into talking about things too much, I just like to let it happen.'

While Slash had been answering the phone I had picked up a copy of *RIP* magazine, with Axl on the cover, which I'd found lying on the carpet in a heap of newspapers and magazines underneath the coffee table. Inside, the singer talked frankly and quite wilfully about a number of controversial topics; particularly drugs, listing heroin as his favourite, though admitting you had to be 'careful'.

'There's some stuff about drugs in there I wish he hadn't said.' Slash chuffed intently at his cigarette when I mentioned it. 'Because, I

73

mean, at this point in time, being that we have such a bad reputation as it is and having run-ins with the cops all the time, I just don't think it's a good idea.' Slash admitted he was paranoid that a fleet of black-and-whites were gonna show up on his doorstep one night – or more likely early one morning – and raid the place, just for the hell of it, just to show who was really boss.

'Because of quotes like that, it's really gotten to the point where everybody's sort of very wary of the police. Just everyday living could be . . . you never know what could happen. Did you know the Feds are after Sam Kinnison?' Slash explained in hushed tones how the Hollywood-based comedian was being hounded by the FBI, who, he said, were determined to pin something – anything – on Kinnison because of certain 'controversial' statements he'd made to the press in interviews and certain 'outlandish' scenes from his live stage act which, in the Bureau's view, were far too 'pro-drugs' and likely to subvert the nation's youth etc etc blah blah blah . . . The upshot being, according to Slash, that Kinnison now had to watch his back wherever he went.

'Anything to do with drugs, you have to watch it,' he said seriously. 'And we're prime targets. Luckily I'm not in West Hollywood any more, so that helps. But as far as I'm concerned you just don't say anything about drugs – just don't talk about them.'

It's funny, I said, how no one mentions the music in connection with Guns N' Roses any more. The public – the media – demanded more from them than that now, it seemed; they had a 'legend' to live up to. Which was why, apparently, no one from the band was doing interviews any more. At least, not at present.

'I've gotten to the point where I've gotten to understand what the press and media are all about. Some people are serious hounds for the dirt to the point where you just sit there and look at them and you just see them as pathetic. Then there are the ones who are a little more subtle, and they just want to have something interesting to write down. It's different. I tend to be pretty calm about it. I sort of take the assholes with the nice guys and just try to, like, weed them out. It doesn't shock me any more, though. There's nothing left that's shocking about it. I can understand why somebody wants to write stuff like that because it makes for interesting reading, and interesting reading makes for decent sales.

One particular magazine – a doyen of establishment rock 'n' roll in America and self-styled arbiter of good taste – had recently put Guns N' Roses on its cover for the first time. The story within was predictable enough fare, littered with various pronouncements on such things as Axl's 'mood swings', and peppered with the buzzwords 'sex', 'drugs' and 'violence'; the band captured mid-flow on the road with Aerosmith the previous summer. 'I mean, it was basically focused on Guns N' Roses' chemical intake, and violence, sex, groupies and all those sorts of things,' Slash said with dismay. 'The guy who wrote the article was on the road with us for a while on the Aerosmith tour, and there was a lot of other things going on. But he used quotes that were, like, just made in passing, just bits of conversation and somehow he managed to pull them out of context and put them in the article the way he wanted. It was just me going. "Oh, you know . . . blah blah blah", it was a conversation, it wasn't part of the interview. But he managed to take that and put it in the magazine. It was sort of a drag to read that and see how you can be had so easily,' he said with an exasperated shrug.

Reading it myself, I said, it struck me the guy already knew what kind of story he wanted to write – he just needed the quotes to colour the picture in a bit.

'Yeah,' Slash agreed. 'You can't really trust them. You sort of, like, want to, you really want to. But when you've got a journalist with you and you've sort of taken him into your confidence and you've allowed him into your surroundings, it's only because you think you can trust him, you think maybe he's cool. So you expose stuff to him that normally you wouldn't expose, and it's a drag when one of those guys turns round and kicks you in the ass and makes you feel like a fool.

'I'm not totally anti-press, though,' he was swift to reassure me. 'The only reason we're not doing any American press at the moment is because so much American press has been done, we don't want to get to the point where we're over-exposed. We don't want people to burn out on us. It's got to the point lately where we're almost on cereal boxes. The magazines are gonna put out stuff on their own anyway, they really will. They make up shit all the time. We just have to lay back a bit. Which is cool, 'cos I don't really feel like talking to anyone right now. I feel I sort of have to get my life in order. Try and, try and . . . I don't know.' He pushed the hair from his eyes. 'Just try and get comfortable living off the road.'

He got up to fix some more drinks. He didn't look very comfortable, I called after him – hidden away in his house in the hills, cursing the phone when it rang, probably wondering why when it didn't . . .

'I don't know,' he said, returning from the kitchen. 'I'm at a point where more and more I'm starting to get comfortable. Because it's obvious, whether I like it or not, that we're gonna be here till the next record's finished. There's nothing I can do about it,' he said, dropping back down onto the armchair. 'So if that's the case I've got no choice. I might as well, like, adjust . . .'

Meantime, while Guns' Roses languished in the rehearsal studio 'getting it together', everybody else was lining up trying to steal their thorny crown away. Or at least trying to come out with a semi-credible version of their own – Poison, Bon Jovi, Ratt, Motley Crue, all had now toned down the make-up drastically and allowed their stubble to show through. In fact, they'd made a point of it in all their latest press shots and videos. Slash had not been slow to make the connection either.

'The cool thing is, I think that's great, 'cos it's like we've broken new ground for rock 'n' roll. Most bands weren't really doing anything like that before we came along, before we broke through. Everybody was doing very pretentious sort of formularized stuff. Formula rock. Then we came out and it sort of broke that mould. So now after everybody else's album has come out, we get to come out with something that is gonna be us but different again,' he boasted. 'Lots of acoustic stuff, lots of really hard-edged shit, some experimental stuff . . . 'Cos time has gone by, but we're just gonna do whatever it is we feel like doing. People might expect only one particular thing from us – it might be completely different from that, though. Which is cool, sort of like turn the corner on everybody, you know what I mean? I'm really excited by it.'

And so, it would seem, were a lot of people; not just the fans, but pundits inside the music industry as well. Which was rare – especially for a so-called 'heavy metal' band. For example, the manager of U2 had recently gone on record as saying he thought Guns N' Roses were 'the most important thing to happen for years'. How did Slash react to a statement like that?

'Well, I'll tell you, there's a weird thing that happens, for me, anyway. It's like, certain compliments come from different people and I take them in different ways. Like getting voted best guitarist in a magazine like *Kerrang!* – that is like one of the all-time greatest compliments for me! I mean, that's something that's real, that you can see. Now Gibson say they want to put together a Slash model Les Paul, with a special Slash pick-up and shit like that. That, to me, is another amazing compliment. It actually means something to me, you know?

'But instead of letting it go to my head, the way that I feel about it is, like, I really don't see my playing as really being worth that. I put it down to record sales and because it's hip to like Guns N' Roses at this time. It would be a real joke for me to go, "Oh, wow, I'm the best guitarist in the world!"' 'cos that's just not true. Although I do like the playing on *Appetite*, I think it does have some feel to it. I would hope I'm better now, though,' he said, sticking his nose back in his glass. 'Ultimately, when I get a real big compliment it gives me the energy and the motivation to play my ass off on the next record, so that I can at least prove to myself that I'm worthy of it. And also, to, er . . .'

Prove you're not a flash in the pan?

'Yeah, exactly. It's like, all this attention and energy devoted to one album, it's *scary*. It's almost like this one album has taken us as high as you can possibly go – on one fuckin' record! So you've gotta fuckin' look out, you know? You can't be complacent. I told Gibson I won't let the guitar come out, or the pick-ups, until this next record is out and the tour starts. Because we could be given all this great stuff and not even come out with a second album. Then I'd feel like a real putz, wouldn't I?'

I had a notion that part of the reason why Slash complained about the relative constraints of his own peculiar stardom was because he was desperate not to let it appear as though any of it had gone to his head.

And nor would it; he was firm on that score. 'It's just that people always focus in on the predictable stuff. Like, Duff hasn't gotten anywhere near enough recognition as a bass player, nobody ever talks about how good a guitar player Izzy is. People notice me and Axl a lot 'cos we're out there at the front. We're highly recognisable and all that shit. But Duff is like one of the best bass players in rock 'n' roll. Duff is an *awesome* bass player, and he doesn't get any recognition for it at all! So it becomes obvious to me, it's not so much how good a player you are, it's how cool you are.

'And you have to understand where all that's coming from. There are people I know that walk around believing their own hype. Then all of a sudden it turns to the next flavour of the month and they get left standing there looking on wondering what the fuck happened, you know?'

Slash said he was already mentally preparing for the almost inevitable Guns N' Roses backlash that would begin sooner or later, he felt sure. 'I personally leave room for that to happen, yeah. It's like, we're really big right now, we've sold a lot of records. The next record will be as good as we can possibly make it, so we'll be happy. But whether it will be flavour of the month when it comes out, I don't know and I don't care. Some people might not be as interested, but, you know, so what?'

Back then, in March '89, with *Appetite For Destruction* and *GN'R*

Lies both still clogging up the world's Top Tens, back when you could actually see the legend of Guns N' Roses growing on an almost daily basis, it was difficult to imagine a time when anyone might not be interested.

'I don't know, it does and it doesn't,' Slash said.

Really? Did the whole thing still feel as fragile and as unpredictable as that – that things might just change overnight?

'Yeah. Yeah. Yeah. Definitely. It's happened to enough bands. I mean, look what happened to Aerosmith. They were huge at one point, and then all of a sudden . . .' He snapped his fingers. 'Gone . . . I've said this so many times before, but no matter who you are, one band doesn't make the world go round, and you can't take yourself so seriously to think it does.'

I commented that for me and a lot of other people the last band that generated the same kind of excitement and appeal as Guns N' Roses was probably the Sex Pistols.

'I know what you're saying,' Slash nodded thoughtfully. 'I think maybe we share a lot of the same attitudes. Not necessarily musically, but in what that music represents to the average kid on the street. The Sex Pistols were a brand new concept, though. It wasn't like sort of rehashing a bunch of little things and putting them together and putting it out, exposing it to people,' he pointed out modestly. 'Punk rock was like this whole deal in itself, and it still lives on, you know? I was into the Pistols when I was in school, they were always cool.'

I asked if, having been this far down the road himself now, Slash could relate to why someone like Sid Vicious might go on stage and slash his own chest open with the broken end of a beer bottle somebody in the audience had thrown at him?

'Well, first you have to get into the frame of mind Vicious was in . . .' he said slowly.

Or do the same drugs, I added dryly.

It raised a knowing smile. 'Yeah, right . . . But there's a certain type of physical aggression that you get on stage. Especially for me. Like, you're out there and you have a capacity for pain that you normally don't have. It's because of all that high-strung energy that you get in times of extreme emergency, you know? Pure adrenalin. And it's such a physical thing . . .

'But I would never be at the point of wanting to slash myself. It doesn't interest me. I put up with some pretty intense degrees of pain when I'm on stage some nights as it is. You know, when I've fallen off stage and got back up and kept going. And there's times I've burned myself on stage pretty badly, too. I like to smoke when I'm on stage, right? Well, there's been a lot of times I've been playing with a cigarette between my lips, and I've let it burn all the way down and the hot coal has dropped down my pants.' He pulled a pained expression. 'But when you're playing there is no way you can stop and do something about it. It goes out eventually, but it leaves a scar. Here, do you wanna see?' he enquired salaciously.

'Out there, on tour,' he continued, ignoring the phone which had begun to ring again, 'you get hit by things when you're on stage, you jump into the crowd. It's like, no holds barred, relentless fuckin' rock 'n' roll. To me that's what high-energy rock 'n' roll is all about. I punch my guitar when we play and I come out of shows all bloody . . .'

Axl said something in either the *RIP* interview or the piece in *Rolling Stone*, to the effect that at certain gigs you've done the audience has almost been on the edge of a riot, where he felt personally threatened. He said there was a certain thrill to be had in itself during moments like that. I asked Slash if he agreed.

'Well, I read something in a magazine where I said I liked seeing people in those tense situations, where everybody's about to beat each other up. That I got off on the fact that the band had generated that much excitement, that much energy. But to correct myself on what I *might* have said,' he cleared his throat, 'I don't really want to see anybody beating themselves up, or beating each other up, because crowd violence is not a pretty sight. Any individuals getting hurt at one of our shows is not what it's all about at all. You know, it's a fine line you walk because you do generate that kind of power, where you can get people to go crazy like that. It makes you crazy and it's like the whole world is about to explode. If it gets so intense, though, that someone's gonna get hurt, then you have to stop the show. Donington, of course, being the ultimate example of one of those times . . .

'And there was a gig we did with Aerosmith at a place in upstate New York. After we got off stage, the medics booth outside, where they take all the casualties, was just loaded with kids. It was like, man, they were fuckin' dropping out there! I remember back to when I used to go to gigs. I'd go to festivals and it was heavy. You have to be strong. It's sort of like you against the rest of them. For each individual person it's like that, because when the whole crowd sways you have to hold onto your own and go with it. It's rough, and that's what came back to me when I saw the kids in the medics booth.'

79

I said I could just imagine the teenage Slash as the typical rabble-rousing headbanger, right down the front of the gig, fist in the air . . . Was he?

'No,' he said, stubbing out his cigarette and dispelling all my preconceptions in one fell swoop. 'I was always calm and I'd stand there and watch the band, 'cos I was really into it. But I go to Slayer gigs now, or Megadeth gigs and get a little drunk and go and slam-dance down the front and, like, dive into the photographers' pit. I have a ball doing it, and that's pretty violent. You just do it for an hour till you're dripping. I remember going to a Ramones gig in New York and just jumping right into the pit. It was intense . . .'

Didn't it concern him that behaving like that in public was almost an open invitation to the one asshole in the room in any given public situation just itching to put themselves up against a member – any member – of the most dangerous band in the world?

'Not when I'm in that state, no . . .' A smile flickered then died on his lips. 'I think that as a concept, though, yeah, it's popped into my head a couple of times, when I've been sitting round the house wondering. You know, there's been things that we've said recently that I realise could offend some people . . .'

Which brought us on to the still unresolved controversy over the lyrics to 'One in a Million'. Slash, clearly, had his own misgivings about Axl's choice of words, though he said he was prepared to defend the singer's right to say them if he really felt they were necessary.

'There's a line in that song where it says, "Police and niggers, get out of my way . . ." that I didn't want Axl to sing,' Slash said, choosing his own words carefully now. 'I didn't want him to sing that but Axl's the kind of person who will sing whatever it is he feels like singing. So I knew that it was gonna come out and it finally did come out. What that line was supposed to mean, though, was police and niggers, OK, but not necessarily talking about the black race. He wasn't talking about black people so much, he was more or less talking about the sort of street thugs that you run into. Especially if you're a naïve mid-western kid coming into the city for the first time and there's these guys trying to pawn this on you and push that on you . . .

'It's a heavy, heavy, *heavily* intimidating thing for somebody like that. I've been living in Hollywood for so long I'm used to it, you know? But I didn't want the song to be taken wrong, which always happens.'

The trouble was, a lot of people did take the song 'wrong' – indeed, still do. And it was going to take a lot more than just Slash's vague assertion that the word 'niggers' could be applied to any number of unsavoury characters regardless of their race, before the majority who were, and remain, offended by that song would be prepared to consider it otherwise. What about the 'immigrants and faggots' that come to 'our country and spread some fuckin' disease'? What was the song supposed to be saying to those people, I asked?

'Yeah,' he said grimly. 'I know, but in the context of the song those are the character's true feelings – his mind is just blown away by what he sees. But there's been a couple of instances where I've decided I was gonna do like an international press release to try and explain what some of this shit is about. Then I thought, no, fuck, that's a waste of time . . .

'But that kind of thing does bother me. Me, in particular. I mean, I'm part black. I don't have anything against black individuals. One of the nice things about Guns N' Roses is that we've always been a people's band. We've never segregated the audience in our minds as white, black or green, you know? But with the release of "One in a Million" I think it did something that I don't think was necessarily positive for the band, and it put us . . .' he threw up his arms, grasping for the right words.

In a doubtful light, I suggested?

'Right, right . . . whenever given the chance I try and say my piece about that, because it really isn't . . . It doesn't even have to be about blacks. The term 'nigger' goes for Chinese, Caucasians, Mexicans . . . blacks too, sure. But it's just like a type of people that, you know, are street dealers and pushers. And that's what it's supposed to mean,' he repeated. I wasn't sure who Slash was trying to convince the most: me or himself. 'It's definitely something to attack us with,' he went on, still wrestling with it. 'It's a bona fide, real thing that they can actually say, you know, "Well, what about that?"'

Presumably, I enquired, Axl would argue that it was OK to make a statement like that on the grounds of 'artistic licence'?

'I guess . . .'

But Slash didn't agree?

'Personally, no. I don't think that that statement served any good. I think that should have been kept at bay altogether. But Axl has a strong feeling about it and he really wanted to say it. But then . . . God forbid that any of us should get arrested and end up in county jail. Can you imagine?' he shuddered. '"Yeah, that's the guy who wrote that song!" You could be in some serious trouble with some of the guys in there. Much more trouble than just the cops.

'Actually, that dawned on me a few days ago . . . We're always in trouble with the police, that's nothing new. And, you know, we're not the only band to ever say something derogatory about the police. But there's a point where you do things that make a statement, that are cool, and there's another point where you do things that just aren't necessary and you're just asking for trouble. To ask for trouble and to intentionally put yourself in a position like that, to me, is not cool. As an artist you're expected to make statements. But you're supposed to make statements that make sense and come across clearly. You don't want to make statements that are so, you know, so blatantly out of proportion, so blown out of proportion that it's ridiculous, no subtlety in them at all.

'My mom – who is black, right? – was in Europe and I talked to her on the phone a little while back, it was the first time we talked for ages. And I asked her if she'd heard the EP yet and she told me, no. But my little brother was out there, and when he came back he told me yeah, she had heard it. But she was so shocked that she didn't know what to say to me on the phone. I thought about that and I thought, you know, I can understand that. So, ultimately, I can't say . . . there's nothing that I can say in the press that's gonna cover it up.'

One thing was for sure, the public recriminations had already begun in earnest; from the press, from other musicians, from the fans themselves. (Shortly after this interview took place Guns N' Roses were unceremoniously dumped from the bill of an AIDS benefit event they had agreed to appear at in New York.)

I recounted the controversy that still raged over a comment Joe Elliot, the singer of Def Leppard, was quoted as having made on stage in El Paso in 1983, concerning some 'greasy Mexicans' in the audience. And that how, on Leppard's 1988 tour of America, a show had nearly been cancelled one night in New Mexico when somebody in the audience was spotted wielding a small pistol just before the band came on stage. They held up the show for forty-five minutes before the security guards located the kid and arrested him. They never found the gun, though. He'd ditched it before the guards got to him. And that was after the band had spent the previous five years apologising for a quote which, according to Joe, was little more than a bad joke taken completely out of context.

'That's harrowing.' Slash narrowed his eyes. 'It sort of makes me think about how, yeah, you can say things, you know, that you feel need to be said. But at the same time you have to really think about what you're saying. So that it's not taken, you know . . . I mean, the band has so far probably made so many statements that we could have just about everybody after us.'

There was another loud ringing. Not from the phone this time: it was the doorbell. My watch said it was 2.48 a.m. Izzy had arrived. He pranced into the room like a man trying to navigate a minefield, floppy cap yanked down over his eyes, cigarette smouldering between thin pale lips, the face and the hands as grey as a ghost's. He had four or five people with him; one of them, Billy Squire, had once been a well-known rock star himself – back in '83, '84. Which was about the last time Billy had had a hit record.

Pretending not to notice the tape-recorder, Izzy spun on his heel and made straight for the kitchen. He'd been to the house before and knew where most of the goodies were stashed. Slash showed the rest of his 'guests' – most of whom he'd plainly never met before – downstairs to a separate den where he told them they could drink and 'hang out until I get done with this shit'. His concentration broken, Slash picked a bright cherry red Gibson out of its case and stood there cradling it against his hip for a moment while Izzy fixed drinks for himself and his friends in the kitchen.

'You got any more vodka?' Izzy called out.

Slash pretended not to hear and started talking about the guitar. 'It's a nice guitar . . . Gibson sent it to me. But like all my new guitars I have to have it taken apart and refurbished. I don't like stark-looking brand new guitars, I just don't like 'em,' he mumbled, strumming chords aimlessly, silently, unplugged.

'It's all right!' called Izzy from the kitchen. 'I found it . . .'

Slash sat back down with the guitar; continued strumming. 'Anyway, Gibson are doing a limited edition Slash Les Paul. This one's sort of what it will look like, only I'm gonna make it more of a blood red with more of the black hardware and stuff. It's gonna be a really good looking Les Paul . . .'

'Yeah, and it's gonna have an Afro on top,' cracked Izzy, returning to the room carrying a tray with glasses and some bottles on it.

Slash ignored that, too. Izzy disappeared down the stairs muttering to himself.

Slash told me a story about how he and Izzy had been asked to interview Keith Richards for a magazine – he said he couldn't remember which magazine. 'I don't know what they had in mind.' He looked baffled. 'I wasn't interested. For some reason people are always trying to put us together with them . . . the Stones. There's even talk of us . . . oh well,' he began, then thought better of it. 'Oh, that's it, I didn't say anything . . . Forget that, OK?'

I shrugged. OK . . . but forget what? In retrospect, it's clear now Slash was referring to the offer the Guns N' Roses office had already received from the Rolling Stones to open the show for them when they hit LA on their comeback tour of the States later that year. I was puzzled, but I let it go. From elsewhere in the house came the sound of guitars and singing. Izzy and Billy had obviously wasted no time in getting acquainted.

Slash appeared to cock an ear to the distant hum, frowned, then got up and padded back to the kitchen to see if they'd left him his bottle of Jack. They had. He returned with it in his hand, sat down again, and started talking about how he'd like to get clean out of LA for a while.

And go where, I asked?

'I don't know . . . just out. I'd like to go to England again . . .' He never did make that Christmas trip over there he'd talked about the last time we spoke. 'I know, but I really wanna play there again, too.'

Why? What was this thing he had for England – for the British audiences?

'Let's put it this way, for me personally, and for Izzy – I can speak for Izzy, I know he feels the same way – but there's playing the States, you know, which is great and all. But then there's going over there and playing, and that's the ultimate. The British crowd is so fuckin' balls out! That, to me, is the epitome of what the rock 'n' roll gig is all about – packing up your gear and going over to England . . .'

He looked so long-faced and sincere as he said this I couldn't help but laugh. For someone like me – born in England – the 'epitome of what the rock 'n' roll gig' was 'all about' had nothing to do with going to England. Quite the opposite: it had everything to do with escaping from the place . . . I tried to explain this but Slash looked unconvinced.

'No, man, seriously . . . if you can be good in England, if you can go to England and be well received, you can play anywhere else in the world, you know that I mean? The fact that we've won so many awards from the magazines over there this year is pretty eye-opening for us. It just makes me feel like they feel the same way about us as we do about them. And yet it seems like out of everywhere that we've played we've sort of cut England short. We haven't given it enough. Just that tour two years ago which, apart from a couple of shows, I thought was pretty half-assed. When the next record comes out, we are adamant about going to play in England first . . .'

Izzy re-appeared in the room, searching, he said, for Slash's twelve-string guitar. The phone rang again and I turned the tape-machine off and got ready to leave, thinking, 'When the next record comes out,' indeed. And when would that be? Not tonight, that was for sure. As we said our goodbyes at the door, Slash's last words to me that night were: 'I'm really not in the mood for company tonight . . .'

I drove back into West Hollywood, grabbed a few hours' sleep, got up again, showered and breakfasted on some solids for a change. Then the phone rang and it was Slash. It was 11.30 a.m.

'What are you doing?' he asked.

'I just got up,' I replied. 'What are you doing?'

'Oh, I'm still at it,' he said with a throaty chuckle that made me think of sandpaper and glue. 'Izzy and Billy are still here and everybody's going strong . . .'

'I thought you weren't in the mood for company?' I said.

'Ah, shit . . .' he croaked and we changed the subject.

FIVE

New Year in Hollywood

JANUARY 1990

New Year's Eve in Los Angeles; a house in West Hollywood. Just minutes to go till midnight and the place was already filling up with freaks of all persuasions: writers, musicians, publicists and managers; agents, designers, chauffeurs, go-fers and professional bottle-openers; wives, girlfriends, boyfriends and friends of . . . friends. It was a desultory gathering and the drinking was fierce. Rudy Sarzo, the bass player from Whitesnake, wandered about – tanned, affable – cuckooing from one conversation-in-progress to another, clutching a glass of champagne in one hand and his pretty champagne-blonde wife in the other.

David Lee Roth's manager, Pete Angelus, was holding court in the kitchen, close by the stocks of still-unopened bubbly, his suave Italian-American features creased into a permanent wolf's grin as he entertained a tight circle of nodding, appreciative faces with another of his absurd and funny little stories; things 'you probably won't believe, but . . .' Meanwhile, back in the lounge, Slash sat slumped in a chair in the corner of the room, shaggy hair pulled down over his eyes, trying not to look too famous; a saucer-eyed teenage beauty queen he'd met at the China Club earlier that same evening balanced on one knee; a bottle of champagne, two fluted glasses and the inevitable ashtray placed on a small table by his side – laid back, but not laid out. Not yet . . .

There were two toilets on the premises and both were impossible to get into all night. People just seemed to emerge from one or other of them from time to time, closing the door shut tight behind them. They would exit in twos and threes, gagging and spluttering and waving their arms in the air as they stumbled back into the room, grasping at things no one else could see. I was pondering all this, holding onto myself and wondering if anyone would notice if I pissed in the pool, when Duff McKagan came stumbling over and grabbed me by the shoulders.

'Man, man . . .'

What?

'Man . . .' He shook his head dolefully. 'I can't talk about it right now but I just had the *worst* Christmas,' he said, leaning his back to the wall. 'But I do wanna talk with you . . . maybe in a couple of days, huh?'

Sure, I told him, why not? Duff seemed to relax, satisfied for the moment, his eyes fixed on a space about two inches above my head. I took a good look at him. At a glance, he looked fine, just like his pictures . . . tall (bottled) blond in faded 501s squeezed into tight black leather chaps, heavy black motorcycle boots, black cotton shirt undone to the stomach and a battered blue denim jacket with the sleeves sawn off. You could see the ladies' eyes flash like traffic signals every time Duff appeared in the room. But looking at his face close up he wasn't such a pretty sight. The corn-coloured hair was lank and greasy; the pink cherubic features pale and unshaven. His eyes were the shade of deep red eyes go when they've been up all night drinking, or crying. Or both.

We stood there and talked for a while and Duff told me that he had, in fact, just split up with his wife, Mandy. The couple had had a bitter row on Christmas day and Duff had ordered her from the house. 'She told me she hated me and I told her to get out and she did. It was the shittiest fucking Christmas I ever had.' Duff and Mandy had been together for over two years, married for most of that time.

At the stroke of midnight, we had ushered in the new decade the American way – counting down to the chimes on MTV, everybody drowning their gizzards in champagne . . . 9, 10, 11, 12 . . . Whoosh! And there we were suddenly – 19fuckin'90! Who woulda thunk it?

Somebody turned the TV set off and cranked up the tape-deck. I turned around and Duff was standing behind me. We shook hands, attempted to slap each other's backs and only succeeded in spilling our drinks over one another. He left a short while after, accompanied by Slash. Clearly, Duff's mind was on other things. He promised to call. No hurry, I said. If I were him, I thought, considering what he must be going through, I wouldn't call.

Two nights later, however, much to my surprise, Duff did call. Slash was still hanging out with him at his house in the hills, and Duff suggested they might come over and join me for a drink, and did I have my tape-recorder ready because, he said, he wanted to 'get something serious down'.

I got my tape-recorder ready. They arrived in a tan chauffeur-driven limousine at about 10.30 p.m., two wasp-waisted blondes in mini-skirts and high-heels in tow. Duff was in a hurry to talk, he said. To get that 'something serious down' he seemed so anxious for. He was already half-cut, of course, but Duff seemed in considerably better spirits than he had done forty-eight hours before. His divorce, he told me, had been made final that day. Under Californian law, any couple married for under two years can obtain a divorce within seven days – which is exactly the time it had taken Duff to divorce Mandy, once he'd made up his mind to do it on Christmas day.

Understandably, Duff said he was reluctant to discuss the breakdown of his marriage in this interview. 'I will say, though, that I'm happy now about the way things turned out. The marriage wasn't going anywhere. We hadn't been happy for a long time . . . We tried, it didn't work, end of story. All I'm thinking about now is going back in the studio and starting work on the new album. And then getting back on the road. There's a reason for everything, I think. Good or bad. And what with everything coming up that the band has to do maybe it's better that I'm on my own right now . . . I certainly feel better already,' he snorted, twirling his glass.

It had been nearly a year since I had last interviewed Slash, and despite the apparent inactivity of the band during that time – exactly five gigs and still no sight of the much-touted second Guns N' Roses album on the misty horizon – there was still a lot to talk about.

In April, the band had put in a guest appearance at that year's Farm Aid concert in Indiana, along with such pillars of the rock establishment as Bob Dylan and event co-organiser, John Cougar Mellencamp, where they also unveiled a brand new number – the first new song to be added to the set for over two years – 'Civil War', for which Axl donned a ten-gallon hat and shades to sing. Halfway through '89, combined sales for both *Appetite For Destruction* and *GN'R Lies* had reached in excess of ten million copies in America alone, and, in June, *Rolling Stone* put Axl on its cover. It was the first major interview Axl had granted that year, but in order to get it *Rolling Stone* had had to agree to allow *RIP* journalist Del James and photographer Robert John – both close friends of the singer's since the early days of the band – to submit the only stories and pictures the magazine would be allowed to use. Then, in September, as Slash had indicated they might, Guns N' Roses played second-fiddle to the reactivated Rolling Stones over four nights at the mammoth 70,000-capacity Los Angeles Coliseum.

The controversy that had continued to dog the band all year over the inflammatory lyrics of 'One in a Million' again reared its ugly head when Vernon Reid – guitarist of all-black rockers Living Colour, who were third on the bill at the Stones' shows – made a short speech from the stage of the Coliseum the first night, to the effect that anybody who called somebody else a nigger – whatever the situation, but particularly, Reid made clear, in the mass-media context of a popular song – was promoting racism and bigotry, no matter how hard they tried to explain it away. The inference was obvious and large sections of the Coliseum crowd stood on their seats and cheered and whistled, applauding loudly.

Then Guns N' Roses came on for their say and Axl trumped everybody by announcing mid-set that this would be his last appearance with the band as too many of its members had been 'dancing with Mr Brownstone', a thinly-veiled reference to heroin, directed, it later transpired, at Slash and Izzy and Steven, who had indeed been sliding back into their bad old ways during the long hiatus from active duty, either touring or recording.

The scene backstage after the show was one of utter pandemonium. Like the boy who cried wolf, nobody was really sure Axl would carry out his threat. But then, nobody was really sure he wouldn't. However, after extracting firm promises from Slash, Steven and Izzy that they would clean up their act straight after their stint with the Stones – and with the added condition that Slash make an announcement from the stage saying as much, which he did, a little red-faced but courageously, nevertheless – Axl was back treading the boards of the Coliseum the following night, and Guns N' Roses had themselves another front page story to sell, bigger and certainly more sensational than anything Mick Jagger and his media wizards would cook up during the Stones' intended high-profile fortnight in LA.

Since then, however, all had seemingly gone quiet again on the Guns N' Roses front. Now I was back in LA, I wanted to know why. Taking a bottle of vodka out of a paper bag and helping himself to glasses and mixer, Duff followed me out to a back room where we would be able to talk in private, leaving Slash to entertain the girls. (Poor guy.)

Duff began by promising that this wasn't going to be 'one of those regular fuckin' rock star bullshit type interviews. Just man to man fuckin' talk here,' he gurgled, an unlit cigarette dangling from his mouth.

I remarked that this was the first time I had actually interviewed anyone from Guns N' Roses other than . . .

'Slash and Axl?' he interrupted. 'The big boys, you mean?' he sneered.

Well, yes, but what did he mean by 'the big boys'? Was that really how Duff felt about them?

'No, man,' he shook his head and grinned. 'It's a joke . . . it's all a joke. It's just that they're – and they'd be the first to admit it – they're the cartoon figures of the band. Whether they like it or not, and I think most times not, they're focused on because Axl is the singer and Slash is like this fucking guitar player, and they're both fuckin' amazing, you know? I don't blame magazines and shit for wanting to get their clutches into them, 'cos they're both so fuckin' great! I mean, Slash . . . he's untamed!' he hollered, waving his glass around. 'And when was the last untamed guitar player – Hendrix? I'm not comparing him to Hendrix, though . . .'

Wasn't that the very reason – beyond the music, beyond the hype – why so many young people felt such a powerful attraction to Slash and Axl, or indeed all of Guns N' Roses: that, as Duff put it, 'untamed quality' to the band?

'Yeah, it's a *very* untamed situation, man.' He laughed out loud again. 'Still to this day, to this minute! But the whole band, we love each other. We call each other every day – I just talked to Axl on the phone before I came out tonight. You know, we care for each other and we always take care of each other . . .'

Just then Slash stuck his head around the door and informed us that he was taking the limo and the girls over to Fat Burgers to get something to eat and did Duff or I want him to bring anything back for us. We thanked him but said no, we were fine as we were.

'OK,' said Slash, pausing at the door. 'By the way, Duff, man, can you, like, loan me some money? I forgot to bring any with me . . .' he smiled sheepishly.

'Sure, but I've only got a hundred-dollar bill,' said Duff, already reaching for his wallet.

'That'll do,' said Slash, stashing the proffered note in his back pocket.

'Just bring me the change,' murmured Duff, but the guitarist had already skidaddled, the door banging shut behind him. 'All right . . . where were we?' Duff ignored his glass and went straight for the vodka bottle, put it to his lips and took a long haul. Then he set it back down again, lit a cigarette, picked up his glass and took a sip from it. 'I mean, this band of ours is very volatile,' he said without skipping a beat. 'But it's not as volatile as it's made out to be in the press – not at all! It's like we're a family . . .'

I decided to cut the crap and get straight to the point, as they say in all the best pot-boilers. The date today was 2 January 1990, and the burning, indeed only, question on the minds of their fans now was: what the hell did Guns N' Roses do all last year? Why hadn't they finished the new album yet? More to the point, why hadn't they even *started* the new album yet?

'We're going into the studio on the 15th of this month . . .' Duff began uncertainly.

OK, I said, but why were they only starting the thing now? Whatever happened to 1989? Apart from the four shows in LA with the Stones and the one-off Farm Aid appearance, what had the band been doing the rest of the time – sitting on their hands?

'Well . . .' he spread his hands out like a dealer showing the mark a clean deck. 'Well . . .' he paused, searching the walls with his eyes for the words. 'Well . . . OK, here's the deal. We've always had enough songs, right? But we went to Chicago – Slash and myself and Steven went there – to try and make a start on the songs. And we waited for Axl and Izzy, but Axl had some reasons for not coming out – he was just waiting for us to do our trip as musicians – and Izzy . . . Izzy was having a hard time with life at that point and was just travelling the world. So we sat in Chicago for three months, the three of us, and kinda got suicidal. But at that point we also got a lot of shit done. So if people are gonna ask, have these guys lost their fuckin' edge, I'd have to say no, we've *gained* a lot more edge.

'You know, before we did the last record we were down, no money, going through all this shit. Now it's like a whole different bunch of shit to deal with. You got people who want to sue you, you got people who want to fight you, you can't go to clubs . . . I got in a fight New Year's Eve, just 'cos some guy wanted to fuck with me,' he said, the expression on his face incredulous. 'Check it out, it was my first night out since I busted up with my wife and all I wanted to do was have a good time. We were there to see Bang Tango. But within twenty seconds this guy comes up to me and says, "Where are you from?" I said I live here, you know. He said, "Well, don't ever touch me again!" I mean, I haven't even been near the guy, I've just walked through the door!' The eyes, still bloodshot and swollen, were almost popping out of his head.

'I just saw red all of a sudden, 'cos of the shit I've been going through.' He lowered his voice to an awed croak. 'I turned to my friend Del and said, "Hold my wallet for me, please." Then I turned back to this guy – and this guy was big, man – and I just went HUUURRGG! And I fuckin' hit the guy.' He demonstrated, standing up and aiming a huge, out-swinging right hook to the jaw of an imaginary opponent. 'It's the first time I've ever seen it in real life, but his eyes went cross-eyed, like in a movie, and then he went down . . .' He gave a little chuckle, then sat back down again. He picked up his cigarette. 'Actually, it's a horror having to deal with shit like that all the time.'

I asked Duff if he ever took a bodyguard with him when he went out at night?

'Fuck, no!' he baulked, as though his honour were at stake even answering such a question.

In the light of events like the most recent example at the China Club, though, didn't Duff think he should consider taking some form of security out with him at night?

'No way!' He looked insulted. 'I'm just a normal guy, man . . .'

Not any more, I said.

'But I am,' he insisted, all piss and vinegar now.

All right, I conceded, but he was a very famous normal guy now and that made him different from most.

'So?' he glared at me.

So, it made him an easy target for the dickheads out there . . .

'So they're dickheads and I'm not! The next morning they'll wake up and know they're a dickhead. And the next day I'll wake up and feel sorry I got in a fight and that's that. I don't use security – fuck that,' he scowled. 'I don't believe in that shit.' Duff admitted, though, that the amount of attention he received now did actively stop him going out sometimes.

'Mmm, it does. But I've gotten used to it . . . There was a period once of about a week where I got into three different fights. One guy started one just because he wanted to show off to his girlfriend. Now it's question of do I want to walk in and deal with being Duff McKagan.' He puffed out his cheeks. 'But if they are going to be that much of a dickhead, OK, fine. I can ditch a fuckin' hit, and I can hit 'em back! If he's gonna be such an asshole then that's his problem, not mine. I never did that to anybody when I first moved here to LA. I never thought of going up to David Lee Roth if I saw him down the Troubadour and telling him I was gonna kick his ass, you know? I just wouldn't have thought of it . . . These guys who do are just assholes. Fuck them.'

'The one I feel sorry for the most,' said Duff, 'is Axl. He's such a huge figure now . . . I mean, what does *he* do when he wants to go to the shopping mall – put on a baseball cap backwards and wear shades? That's what he wears on stage, man, you know . . . So I feel sorry for him. But it's all the same, the edge is still there. It definitely is still there, man.' Duff looked me hard in the eye. 'It is not lost. I mean, this new album, the songs are just so . . .'

What?

'Well, there's so many of them for a start. We have songs for days . . . We have thirty-five fuckin' songs written for this next fuckin' album! It may be a double-album, I don't know. None of us knows yet.'

But were they thirty-five songs they were proud of, or thirty-five songs that might or might not work once the band finally – if ever – got back into a recording studio?

'No, we have thirty-five songs that we are proud of.' Duff assured me. 'And I tell you what, man, not to brag, but my bass playing has gotten so much better. Slash's guitar playing has gotten immense! And fuckin' Axl's voice has gone from . . . The vocals on the *Appetite* album were great, but he was still a kid back then learning how to use his voice. Now he's like' – he smacked a fist into the palm of his hand – 'he's got it nailed, man.'

Duff pointed to an old Guns N' Roses poster tacked to the wall, circa '87. 'That band right there,' he pointed a ringed finger, 'we were kids trying to be tough fuckin' nuts, right? Now we're like, we know what we want to do and we know we can do it. There's a difference, man. There's a difference,' he repeated almost to himself, gazing up at the wall at his past. 'There's been a big growing period since then . . .' Duff said 1989 had been 'a very tough year for every single person in the band'.

I put it to him that the popularly received wisdom of the time suggested that part of the band's problems the previous year had stemmed largely, if not wholly, from their wholesale use of drugs. That, simply, Guns N' Roses were too out of their heads to get it together any more . . .

He nodded his head impatiently. 'Sure, sure, and maybe at times it's been true. But . . . it's nobody's business but ours. We're a rock 'n' roll band, you know? We'll make the music, man. But if I fuck a cow, it's nobody's business, man. It's just nobody's business to fuck with any of that shit!' Duff said touchily. 'But the drugs . . . drugs are bad, I will always be the first to say that. Everybody in this band has had his bouts with drugs, but that's all over now. Before, it would mess with the band; guys wouldn't show up for rehearsal; guys would come to gigs all fucked up. But it's like, that's all over now, it really is.' He took another large swallow from the bottle.

I asked about the little 'retirement' speech Axl had made on stage at the first Stones show, citing the fact that too many members of the band had been 'dancing with Mr Brownstone'. Had Duff been aware of what was about to happen?

'Of course not! I was pissed off at him for that, too. But I can say I was pissed off with Axl for doing that because I was not one of the guys that he was talking about. I mean, I just walked into that thing. So I was furious, of course. But the next day we were on the phone together, and you know, it was OK, he explained his reasons for doing it. He was blowing off a lot of steam about a lot of shit. A *lot* of shit. The fact that the band hadn't gotten it together in Chicago, shit like that . . . But yeah, I was mad at Axl, I was pissed off. Then we got on the phone – and that's the beauty of this band – we got on the phone the next day and really got out what was going on. That's what happens with this band, we don't bottle shit up. We just let it out. And sometimes it'll happen on stage.' He grinned. 'It may not have been the right place, but it sure worked!'

Meaning that Slash and Izzy and Steven had now 'cleaned up', I asked?

'Yeah. Slash definitely, he's really fuckin' happening right now. Izzy and Steven too . . . I think, I hope. I mean, we don't know what the fuck's going on. We don't! Axl will tell you the same. I don't know what the fuck's going to happen in the next five minutes in my head! But in this band I consider myself pretty stable.' He smiled broadly. 'I try to make things work musically in the band. I kind of consider myself the musical director, trying to keep everything together. Axl is the word-master and the melody maker. And Slash is the genius of the band . . .'

Slash was the genius of the band? Why?

Duff laughed. 'He's just this fucked up guy that you wouldn't think could . . . I've known the guy since I moved here. I've known him from, like, this kid where I thought, OK, he's just another good guitar player, to, like, this total fuckin' monstrosity that I think he is now! Maybe I'm overplaying Slash, I don't know. But just to me, as a musician, I appreciate him so much, you know? Axl is amazing too, just amazing . . .'

Drink firmly in hand and freshly lit cigarette dangling just-so from his lips, Duff settled back in his seat and began to reminisce about the early days of Guns N' Roses. 'To me, like when we first got together, I wasn't sure about Axl. I was like, he's good but I don't know. But that was when we had those other two cats in the band and the band was not working. But when this band clicked, Axl all of a sudden clicked. It took something finally for him to click and it took something for Slash to click, but when it did it really did . . .'

When did Duff know it was special, though? Could he place the actual turning point?

'OK, here's my story of the whole thing. OK, I moved to LA and I was in a band with Steven and Slash. I hated Steven. He was a real little asshole. He had a double-drum, all these drums and shit, and he was just a little asshole. I love him now to death, but he'll tell you himself, he was an asshole then. We were in a band called Road Crew – not for long, nothing was really happening and I split. After that I got together with Axl and Izzy; they had a band and they said, can you come and play bass for us? It was already called Guns N' Roses, but there was another guy on guitar called Tracii [Guns] and a different drummer [Rob Gardener], and it was a real iffy band. Like, I would hardly show up for rehearsal, and that is not like me. I am always the first guy to show up at rehearsal, the first guy to do everything like that.

'Anyway, I planned a fuckin' tour for us. 'Cos I'd played in punk rock groups all over the country, in punk rock clubs. So I booked us this tour – just up and down the west coast. But Rob and Tracii suddenly chickened out, like, three days before the thing was due to start. Like, "Oh, we don't know if we wanna do it ..."' He screwed up his face like a baby being denied the bottle. 'I was like, fuck you! So we got Slash and Steven in the band at the last minute, and it clicked. We had three days to rehearse and everybody was like, OK, we'll give it a shot ...

'We had borrowed a car to go up to Seattle in, where the first gig was, and we got about a hundred miles out of LA and the car broke down. We had to hitch rides the rest of the way and ... This is an old story, right? But that is when the band really clicked. We all stuck together. We went out and played a shitty first gig; we had no transportation back, and we had to bum a lift with this chick who was a junky. It was horrible,' he recalled with obvious relish.

'After that we knew, OK, this is for real, and about two months later we did our first demo. This guy called Black Randy – he was in a band called the Metro Squad, I don't know if you've heard of them – he put the money up for us to do it, and we recorded it at this little punk rock studio. He has since passed away, this guy, but he gave us the money and we did the demo. Then we just started playing. We did Mondays at the Troubadour; then we were doing Tuesdays. That was like God for us at the time, just opening for bands at the Troubadour. We were all like, wow ... this is it! Then all of a sudden they had bands opening for us. Also, the record labels started coming down. And again, we were like, wow. But we never ... Like, you know, the Chrysalis fuckin' brains came along and said we'll give you guys $750,000, and we just said, yeah, but have you ever heard us play? And they were like, No, but ... So we were like, See ya!

'So there was this little label war, everybody trying to get us to sign – we had a lot of great lunches, I tell ya!' Another broad smirk. 'Finally we went with the record company that really wanted to put something into us and believe in us. And it worked. Everybody was into the kind of record we were making, and everyone dug in and did a good job.

But surely so mundane a reason could not possibly explain the vast scale of the success Guns N' Roses now enjoyed. Geffen Records were recognised as the classiest, bestselling hard rock label in America, and of course they were experts in making and marketing multi-platinum rock albums. But it wasn't every day they released a new band's debut album – let alone an album so inherently uncommercial – then sat back and watched it sell more than ten million copies. Indeed, it was unprecedented in the company's history.

Committed to the band as Geffen had undoubtedly been, surely the level of success Guns N' Roses now flirted with so precariously had little to do with the marketing strategies or promotional hoopla of a shrewd no-chances-taken record company. This, baby, was the real thing . . . wasn't it?

'You wanna know why I think it is?' mused Duff, hunching up in his chair, one long leather-clad leg dangling over the side of the armrest. 'Because Steven is one sort who nobody can really explain. Izzy is another sort that nobody can really explain. Axl is like . . . Axl – who has brought this whole new thing with him that people try to imitate all the time now. And Slash is . . . what? He's a "what?", that's what he is. And there hasn't been a "what?" in years, do you know what I mean? Am I making sense? Basically, it's obvious we're all different kinds of people into different kinds of things. We don't like absolutely everything about each other, we don't agree on everything. But we don't lie about it, and somehow it works.'

People reacted to the honesty?

'Yeah, I think they do. They just look at us,' he squinted his eyes up at the poster again, 'and go, "What!?"'

Who else, these days, would Duff put into that category; who else out there would he say was a genuine "What?"

'Metallica,' he replied unhesitatingly. 'They are definitely a big "What?", you know what I mean? I love Metallica. And I love Faith No More – their guitarist, Big Jim [Martin], he's a "what?", all right. And their singer [Mike Patten], he's a "what?", too! Then you look around and there's very few bands out there that are. There is only a few fuckin' bands now. There's this band and that, there's literally hundreds of bands out there. But where's the fuckin' Small Faces, you know? Where's the new Sex Pistols?'

Maybe they're right here, I suggested. Wasn't Guns N' Roses, in its own way and of its own murky generation, carrying on the same aggressive spirit of the Pistols, the Who, Zeppelin, the Stones et al?

'I don't know . . . I loved the Sex Pistols. I was in many punk rock bands when I was a teenager. I went through that whole thing. The Pistols, the Damned, the Clash . . . But the Pistols had a concept behind what they did, they meant to do it. Malcolm McLaren was the man behind that. And it was Steve Jones who put, like, fourteen guitar tracks on the album. He wanted to make it a really powerful record and God bless him for that. He turned them into a good rock band – on record.

'We play the Pistols album before going on stage some nights,' Duff went on. 'But we also play [seminal LA punks] Fear before going on. We play Prince before we go on. We play Cameo. We play Faith No More, we play Metallica, we play Lenny Kravitz . . . It's just so spread apart now. So for us to say that we're taking after the Pistols is such a cut-off, at this point. It's just such a cut-off. But the Pistols – every rocker who is over the age of eighteen years old owes a fuckin' debt to the Pistols. That is no lie. Like, every rocker in the fuckin' world owes a debt to Hendrix,' he said, raising his glass. 'And every rocker in the fuckin' universe owes a debt to Aerosmith and AC/DC. Now we owe a debt to Fear, we owe a debt to Metallica. We must fuckin' look up to Faith No More. It just goes on and on. It's endless.' He raked at his hair with his hand.

'I must say that Axl has fucking balls,' Duff announced suddenly, thinking aloud. 'I couldn't do shit like that. I do the shit on my bass but I don't have the gift of the fuckin' gab like he has. Axl always knows what to fuckin' say.'

Axl certainly always seemed to have something to say on just about anything and everything – when you finally got hold of him, I said.

Duff smiled. 'I couldn't imagine saying some of the shit he does. It comes straight off the top of his head, too. If it was me I'd go up there and say, "This is another fuckin' song, it's called blah blah blah . . ."' But Axl gets up there and he's like, "I woke up this morning, man, and I really wasn't feeling too good, and I thought back to something that happened to me once . . ." And he just goes on and comes up with something brilliant! Like a brilliant thing that he really means. It's never a story, either, it's always true. I just look over at him some nights and go, "What the fuck?" you know? He's a one of a kind man, all right. There's only a few people can do that. And it takes a lot of balls. He could have been killed at any time or got his ass fuckin' beat, 'cos of the way he is. But he takes that chance, he does not care. He really does not care.'

Didn't that ever make Duff a little scared, too, though? After all, if an audience ever did decide to turn on the band and storm the stage, it's doubtful they would concentrate their attentions solely on the singer . . .

'Yeah, I've thought about it.' He smiled coyly. 'But I won't say it. I will say that if anybody came after Axl and attacked him, I would get right in the way even if it meant getting my head smashed in,' he said grimly. 'Axl would do the same for me, I know it. I've done it for Slash, and if it was Izzy, I'd do it for Izzy. They'd all do it for me, too. That's another cool thing about this band – we protect each other and watch out for each other. If there is something dangerous, though,' he added pointedly, 'it's the shit that's happening over this "One in a Million' crap . . .'

Unlike Slash, Duff didn't appear to have any problems at all with the lyrics to 'One in a Million'. Though again, Duff tended to focus exclusively on the racial aspect.

'For a start, the "nigger" thing,' he began, taking a deep breath. 'Slash comes from a family that is half-black. My family is a quarter black . . . I mean, readers,' he leaned in closer to the tape-recorder mike and yelled, 'LISTEN to EVERY lyric in the song! The song's about Axl coming to LA for the first time on the fuckin' bus. He was a fuckin' green, wet-behind-the-ears white boy, and he was scared to fuckin' death! That is what the song is about and that's it, people can take it the way they want to. Of course, right now they're gonna just fuckin' slag us,' Duff admitted. 'I'd rather not get too much into it, though. If you can't get anything out of it then don't listen, is my message.'

But surely Duff could see why some people would take such offence at some of the lines in the song?

'I can understand some people taking offence to it, yeah. But, ultimately . . . why? All it is, is a tale about life actually in this fuckin' town, downtown LA. OK, it's a white guy telling the tale. So what? That's his story. All it is, is a white kid telling his tale. But I don't want to say too much. Axl's got such a reputation now that of course they're gonna jump all over his ass – he said that dirty word, you know? I mean, check it out, I've been an uncle since I was two years old. My first nephew when I was two was black. It was my sister's kid; she married a black guy. Now I have sixteen nephews and nieces and cousins and shit, lots of which are black, or part black.

'I never heard the word "nigger" until I went to fuckin' school! Until I went to school I didn't know there was a difference between black and white. Then at school you'd see them, the white kids giving a hard time to the black kids. Like, "Fuck you, nigger!" I was like, "Fuck you, you white fuckin' asshole!" Like, why are you calling him a nigger? What does it mean? I couldn't see the difference. So I've always felt very strongly about this. We were in Australia and there's this big skinhead movement down there. Slash and I wanted to come out and make a press statement or something while we there, against the skinheads . . .'

Had the Aussie skins come to any of the shows?

'No. But they were against the Aborigines, and they were against the blacks, and shit. They're so racist you wouldn't believe it. Slash and I are so against that shit. And so is Axl, so is Axl,' Duff was quick to assert. 'He's not prejudiced at all. There is no prejudice in this band. The simple thing about this song is that it is just a tale of what happens to a fucking kid from Indiana – not from London, or San Francisco, but from out of nowhere to the big city – and being scared off his ass. He didn't know the right words to use. So that is all it's about, man.

'Let's stop now,' Duff pleaded, still seeking sanctuary from the vodka bottle. Then touching it off with the obligatory cigarette. 'No more . . .'

One last thing, I pushed my luck. Did this mean that the next time Axl walked through the rehearsal room door with a – for want of a better word – controversial new lyric, the rest of the band would throw up their hands in despair and refuse to consider it?

'Well, that song will never happen again . . .' I thought Duff was going to add the word 'hopefully', but he didn't.

Had they ever played 'One in a Million' live, I wondered?

'We've never done it live, no.'

Would they ever consider performing it live?

'I doubt it.' Duff looked startled by the thought. 'You know, it's been said. That song is that song. I can't see us doing a song like that again. Not because we're too chickenshit to do it, but because there's nothing now in our lives like that. Our new songs are what's going on now . . .'

We allowed the past to fade to black and got onto the future. Duff began to tell me about one of the songs he had written for the new album.

'It's a song I wrote about the press,' he explained bashfully. 'It's called "Why Do You Look at Me When You Hate Me?". It means like, why do you keep writing about us when you already hate us? Why? Why don't they do their job and write about something they think is fuckin' cool instead?' He was on a roll now. 'I don't mind if people hate us after they've seen the gig. But if they hate us before they even come to the gig, why the fuck are they there? So I wrote a song about that . . .

'Slash has got some really fuckin' cool tunes too, which Axl has put some words to. And Izzy's got some really great tunes as well. There's one Izzy's got called "You're Pretty Tied Up". It's actually a factual story about this chick down on Melrose we know, she's like a dominatrix chick, you know? You pay her and you're pretty tied up. It's a great song . . .' He started crooning the title.

'Man, we can't write songs about things we haven't lived through,' Duff continued without taking a breath. 'I can never imagine writing a song about' – he began to sing again – ' "That pool is very shiny/It looks so very nice . . ." I couldn't do that. The fact of the band being so what it is, and the fact that the kids grasp onto it, is because we know what the fuck we're talking about. We lived through that shit, we didn't invent it. You know, like in England the kids go nuts, they're going fucking crazy because over in England it's so stale a lot of times. I mean, I love England, I love London. But the kids just need something to grasp onto. They need a release, you know?

'And we reverted a fucking bunch of kids in America . . . Well, we didn't revert them, we just made them realise that, if I may steal a phrase' – he started to sing again – ' "Heaven isn't too far away". 'Cos it ain't so well here in America. It's not as happening as people think it is. It is good for, like, rock 'n' roll and good times, right? But I'm talking about regular life. Man, I went through the shit just like anybody else. There was a time from about '82 to '83 when I was looking for jobs. I'd take a bus to do a dishwasher job. I was like sixteen or seventeen, and they'd have a forty-year-old man next to me washing dishes too. It's like that all over the country . . .'

Despite having 'one shit fuckin' Christmas', Duff maintained that he now felt 'happier, far more positive' about his and the band's future than he had for some considerable time. 'In the last eight months or so I just wasn't sure if I, or if we, were mentally capable of making the next record. When we made the first record, man, I had one foot like this and one foot like this . . .' He stood up again and planted his boots about five feet apart. 'In those days, man, there was two-inch deep marks where I was dug-in to do this,' he said, swaying gently on his heels. 'I wasn't sure that I could do that again – just dig in and do it. But I've just gone through a bunch of shit in my personal life and now I hope I'm dug in again. I've been hanging with Slash, we've been playing together, and I'm ready again.

'You know, shit has happened in my life.' He collapsed into his seat again. 'But shit happens for a reason, and it happened for a reason in my life and I'm fuckin' happy. I'm so ready to do this fuckin' record, man, I've got callouses all over my fuckin' hands already.' He fanned out the fingers of his left hand for my inspection, and sure enough the tips were blunted by small dark sores. 'I'm just ready to kick fuckin' ass! I wanna go on tour and make people happy. I wanna give a purpose to someone's life,' he announced grandly, smiling like a crocodile and lighting another cigarette. 'No, really. If I can give a purpose to one person's life, that's pretty fuckin' cool by me . . . I mean, how many people can do that to someone else?' he asked, not unreasonably. 'It doesn't happen very often . . . But when it does, you go home at night and you just freak out.'

What about the other side of the coin, though?

'You mean like Donington?'

I nodded.

'Well, obviously that's totally the other side of the coin, but yeah, that was a fucked thing . . .' Duff quieted down for a second and his face went blank. 'It makes me cry – every day, if I think about it,' he murmured in a voice that sounded like it came all the way from the bottom of his boots.

Duff said he saw the whole thing from the stage. 'Saw the whole fuckin' event, man! I saw it going down. And we stopped, man. We stopped and screamed, "Back the fuck up!" 'cos we saw the kids going under . . . "Back the fuck up! Back the fuck up!"' he cried, wild-eyed, re-living the moment. 'And the mud was *this* thick, it was about a foot deep, and we saw the kids go under and then some other people came over them. They couldn't tell they were stepping on people, they thought it was just mud.' He pushed his calloused fingers through the lank yellow hair. 'And, man, we were like, this is our fault, man . . . But we were frantic – back up, back up! I was there and I was watching it and there just seemed like nothing we could do except scream at them. I was ready to jump into the crowd, but I was scared to die myself. Maybe that's chickenshit . . .'

I said I thought it was a brave admission, under the circumstances. But did Duff blame himself personally in any way for the tragedy of the two fans' deaths?

'I tell you, Mick, it really crushed us all,' he said, his face like stone suddenly. 'It really crushed us all. We went back to the hotel that night and we were watching the fuckin' news – they didn't know who the kids were yet but one of them had this tattoo. We were just . . .' He drifted into uncomfortable silence. 'At first I felt that it was totally our fault for months and months. I probably will for the rest of my life.'

But why? Realistically, what else could Duff or the rest of the band have actually done to save those kids?

'Well, look at it this way, if we weren't there then maybe it wouldn't have happened. So I've got that to live with for the rest of my life. I don't think it was our fault, in so much as we didn't say step on these two guys. But then again . . . if we weren't there, Mick, if we hadn't caught the plane and missed the gig, maybe two guys would still be living today. That is a big fuckin' responsibility, man. There's a lot of shit that goes on, a lot of responsibility, that just fucks with our heads. I'm still learning how to deal with it, you know? Like, I ride a mountain bike now and I try to, er, just keep my head straight. I hang out with Slash and I . . . er . . . it's difficult, man. It's hard. I went through a lot of shit in my head about Donington. It just gets difficult sometimes . . .' He picked up his empty glass and stared at it.

I did the same.

'On a positive note,' Duff said, 'we may just be a rock 'n' roll band that doesn't know what it's fuckin' doing sometimes, but at least we're honest. I've heard some rumours that we were like this thing that the record company made up to make some money and shit. If anybody believes that, man, then they're fucked . . .'

I don't think anybody could have made you lot up, I smiled.

'Jesus, I wouldn't be in the band if they had,' he chuckled deeply. 'That's why the kids like us. Kids need a band like us. I wish there was more cool bands that sang honestly, from the heart, you know? There's too many fuckin' Poisons, too many Warrants . . . There's just too many MTV bands that just do this thing, you know, with the costumes . . . So they fuckin' do their trip, and I guess that's cool. Maybe the world needs a band like Warrant, I don't know.

'But for us, we can't do that. We just *can't* . . . If we die, if the band itself dies, then at least we did what the fuck we wanted to do, and that's what it's all about. That's what it's always been about to this band.' The cap came off the vodka bottle again. 'I've been playing rock 'n' roll since I was fourteen years old, and I never fuckin' once looked at the possibility of being in a commercial band. I had chances, and I said, fuck you, fuck you and fuck that . . .'

I said that in my opinion Guns N' Roses had a glorious future mapped out in front of them – if they wanted it. The question was how many of them would still be around to see it.

'Yeah, well, I don't think about it like that . . .' He lapsed into another uneasy silence.

I changed tack. How aware was Duff of the legend that had already been built up around the band?

'Again, I try not to think about that too much,' he replied steadily. 'People tell me that but we could go to a bar and hang out all night and talk as just fuckin' dudes, you know that. I play bass in a band, man. That's all I think about. I'm not trying to be falsely modest or any of that shit. That's it. I play in a band I love. Legendary? Fuck that. Legendary's like fucking Hemingway, OK? We're just a rock 'n' roll band and that's all there is to it . . .

'We've got some fucking great guys in the band, though. We've really got some talented fucking people in this band. Great, that's what it's all about. I love to see Slash fuckin' play the blues, man! I just love it and I'm glad other people do too. But legendary? Legendary is fuckin' James Cagney. Legendary is other shit. We are a band who have yet to prove ourselves. We put out one record and one half-assed fuckin' . . .' Duff couldn't keep a straight face any longer and erupted into wild frantic laughter. 'Dude, we haven't done shit!' he hollered. 'I mean, in my book the guys in our band are great and we'll love each other for the rest of our lives. But legendary?' Another coughing fit of laughter.

'OK, here's what it is: you're a musician, you want to do what you want to do and get to the top, right? Well, most musicians will do anything to get to the top, they'll compromise and they'll do what it takes. But we wouldn't do that. We wanted to do what we wanted to do and somehow it worked. And there hasn't been a band like us who has done that since . . . whenever. I'm not trying to brag, I'm being as humble as possible here . . .'

But what of the millions of fans who already believed in the Guns N' Roses legend, the people out there that bought the records and actually lived the dream vicariously through the adventures of the band – had the sheer weight of their expectations begun to tell on Duff and the rest of the band subconsciously, perhaps? And might that be yet another powerful reason why recording for the new album hadn't even begun yet: the fact that after only one album the band already had a past of quite mythic proportions to live up to? Or to live down, even?

'No.' Duff was certain. 'Not for me, anyway. It just doesn't come in there. I love playing live. I love seeing the crowd. I love making the crowd understand where we're coming from. If they don't – cool. If they do, and I really think they do, it's the best. We're lucky. The fans we have really understand where we're coming from, which is important. And there's a certain vibe we get on stage from the fans that makes it fuckin' volatile, man . . . and fun and fucking real.' He laid special emphasis on the last word.

'You know, and people go home and feel this fuckin' explosion. It used to happen to me like that, man. I saw the Clash, and I got home and it was like fuck! What am I gonna do! I had all this energy. I saw the Damned and it was the same thing. They both gave me this thing that I lived on for a long time afterwards – that maybe I'm still living on. The Prince *1999* record, I lived on that record, it gave something to me. It gave me something that I could hold onto . . .'

One of the things, I said, I thought the critics always missed about Guns N' Roses was the band's wonderful – somewhat warped – sense of humour.

'Sure, I agree. We laugh at ourselves a lot of the time. We don't take ourselves that seriously, man, we can't do that. We're just a rock 'n' roll band and there's plenty of times when it's fun.

'This has been a heavy interview but rock 'n' roll is supposed to mean fun and fucking. Get away from all your problems; get away from all that shit and come and have a fuckin' good time! And if you get some idea out of it then think about it. Maybe try to make it part of your life. That's the coolest thing, you know what I'm saying?'

The sound of music and laughter began to emanate from the next room. Slash and the girls were back from their trip to Fat Burgers. Duff looked at his watch, looked at the nearly empty vodka bottle standing on the floor between us, then back up at me. It was time to wrap it up. We ended where we had begun: with the new album. It seemed as though we would never stop talking about it.

'What else do you wanna know?' Duff grinned gamely.

The release date would be nice, I quipped.

'Oh, man . . . I wish I knew that one myself. All I can tell you for sure is that we go into the studio on the 15th.'

Of January? (I was being facetious.)

'Yeah.'

1990?

'No, 1999!' he scolded. 'No, in two weeks. Same studio we recorded the first album in, same everything.'

Same producer – Mike Clink – too?

'Yeah, as far as the basic tracks go. I talked to Axl about this, and he agrees, and so does Slash: the drums and bass on the last record are just so awesome. I loved Steven's drum sound, I loved my bass sound – it's just so round and in your face! So I mean, why change? I'm even using the same old amps and shit I always use.'

For luck?

'No, man, because they still sound so great. They're not old, anyway, they're good amps. It's this whole cabinet I put together.'

And with more than thirty-five songs to choose from – at least according to Duff – were the chances then that the next Guns N' Roses album would be a double?

'OK, here's what it is. It will be a double album – if we can make a double album. If we burn out after, like, fourteen songs then why go on just to make a double album?'

How long did they have the studio booked for?

'It's open-ended.'

Ask a stupid question . . .

'Well, yeah, it's funny because they've already been open for us for about a year . . .'

I thought back to fifteen months before when Slash had also assured me the band would be back in the studio by January . . . 1989.

'We'll get it done,' Duff said seriously. 'Things fall into place – or they don't – for a reason. If we're not doing the record till now then there's got to be a good reason. I always believe in that shit. It's not that I'm one of those fuckin' weirdos, it's just that so much shit has happened to me that there's *got* to be a reason. And even if there's not, it'll work anyhow. It'll work anyhow, fuck it . . .' Duff looked confident.

I asked if the band had come up with a tentative title for the next album yet?

'I think *Girth* or *Heinous* would be a great name for the record,' he smiled. '*Girth* . . .' He ran the movie through his mind. 'We could have special promos of, like, a big dick . . . I don't know, we joke about it but we have actually got this song called "Girth" . . . Well, it's not going to be called "Girth" on the album, it'll get changed, but it's such a heavy song we call it "Girth" for now. It's named after this guy Wes [Arkeen], who writes with us sometimes. He's a real little fucker, right? But his dick, it's only about this long but it's like *this wide*, man! So he's got the girth, right? So we call this song "Girth" . . .'

Speaking of the enigmatic Mr Arkeen, I wondered if he had contributed any of the lyrics to the new material?

'Yeah, we got a song called "Yesterdays" – a great fucking song.

And, er, "Just Another Sunday". Both great tunes that we wrote aeons ago . . . Like, "It's So Easy" Wes and I wrote together, that's what we did for the last record. Axl put about a quarter of the lyrics into that. But this time these songs are almost fully his, I guess, if I remember right . . . Maybe I wrote part of them with Wes and Axl, yeah, whatever. But, yeah, Wes is gonna be with us on this one.'

Given an ideal setting – always highly improbable where Guns N' Roses were concerned, but I let that pass – Duff said he'd like to see the album in the stores by the end of the coming summer. 'The basic tracks could take about three weeks. Stevie and I are really fast, we work real hard together. Then Slash could do his guitars in another three weeks. Axl . . . it's hard to say how his voice holds up, and he's bound to come up with new ideas. So that's already six weeks,' Duff said, already counting the days. 'It'll take a few months, but if we can start touring again by the end of the summer, it'll be great . . .'

I played the game a little longer and asked where the band were likely to start off their next world tour, assuming it did begin that year? (A rash assumption, as it turned out, but by then that hardly came as a big surprise.)

'There's been talk of starting in Europe, just going over and doing all over, 'cos we haven't done Italy and France, places like that, yet. And of course, we'll come over and play England. We've been more faithful to England than any other fucking place in the world, let me tell you.'

I was taken aback by that last statement. Nine shows in two years wasn't a hell of a lot compared to some bands . . .

But Duff was adamant. 'The first three gigs we ever did anywhere outside America was at the Marquee in London. Then what did we do? We came down with fuckin' Faster Pussycat! Then we came back and did Donington. We haven't gone back to any other places like that. We haven't gone back to, like, fuckin' Australia to play all the time. Or Japan. I mean, dude, we love England, it's like our second home there. The kids just really grasped on to us the first time we were there. We were like, wow, you know? 'Cos the place has such a fuckin' tradition of turning out these great bands. You know, I'm not saying we're the next blah blah blah. But then we came along and we were like the next hard rock band the kids really fuckin' went for. Like, this is our band, nobody can take them away from us 'cos they belong to us. That's how we really felt. The food sucks, though,' he added ruefully.

Which seemed as good a place as any to end it. I asked Duff if he had anything else he wanted to say before I turned off the tape-machine?

'Just everybody keep their chin up and fuckin' rock 'n' roll will never die. That's fuckin' all there is to it, man,' he said, reaching for his cigarettes, and jacket. 'If feelings are gonna die,' he added as a parting shot, 'you will die with them, so see ya!'

I threw the empty vodka bottle into the trash can and emptied all the ashtrays. Then I walked outside to stand by the pool and get some air into my sore lungs. It was gone midnight and the moon was up. I stood there watching it sink behind black night clouds and thought about some of what Duff had said.

Something still didn't feel quite right. 'If they're not careful there's never going to be another Guns N' Roses album,' I said to myself doomily. 'Not this year, not next year, nor the year after that.' But that wasn't right either . . .

SIX

Axl 1990

JANUARY 1990

I had to wait a long time for my interview with Axl. But like all the best and the worst things in life, once I got it, I got it good. We had run into each other two or three times since that initial meeting in Manchester two years before – backstage at Donington in '88 and a couple of times more recently at the Cathouse in LA. But Axl had always maintained a certain distance from me and he almost never looked me directly in the eye when he spoke. I had never pursued things further because I knew it would have been pointless. Axl knew all about me anyway – one night at the Cathouse he told me how much he had enjoyed reading 'the continuing adventures of Slash', as he put it, that I had written up for *Kerrang!* from the interviews we had done together. I figured that when he wanted to talk – if he wanted to talk – he'd know where to find me.

He did. It was just a few days after my meeting with Duff. My last night in LA, in fact. I was leaving the next day for London and I had been out for dinner and drunk just enough heavy red wine to give me a good night's sleep before I left for the airport in the morning. The clock by my bed said it was 11.30 p.m. I thought of lambs leaping. There would never be a worse time for him to call. The phone rang. Whatever else you may think of W. Axl Rose, you've got to admit, the kid's got *timing* . . .

Axl was pissed off. Not, thankfully, in the grand manner to which we had now become accustomed: no glass-smashing, no room-wrecking. But he had a bee in his bonnet that he badly wanted squashing, and so what if it was nearly midnight and I had to catch a plane in the morning, why didn't I come over right now and take down some kind of statement? Sleep's for creeps, anyway. Come on, whaddaya say? I never even got to take off my jacket.

Axl lives in a small two-bedroom apartment in a smart security-guarded apartment block in West Hollywood, just a few minutes' drive from where I was staying with friends. He met me at the door dressed simply in faded blue jeans, and a baggy grey sweatshirt with the sleeves rolled up, revealing skinny heavily-tattooed forearms. His wrists were smothered in literally hundreds of silver bangles that clattered noisily every time he moved his hands, which he did a lot, counterpointing every utterance furiously.

His eyebrows were like thunder clouds. 'I can't believe this shit I just read in *Kerrang!*' he scowled, holding up a copy of the magazine, yanked open at a page from a recent interview with Motley Crue. 'The interviewer asks Vince Neil about him throwin' a punch at Izzy backstage at the MTV awards last year.' He began to read aloud in a voice heavy with sarcasm: '"Vince replies, 'I just punched that dick and broke his fuckin' nose! Anybody who beats up on a woman deserves to get the shit kicked out of them. Izzy hit my wife, a year before I hit him.'" Well, that's just a crock of shit,' he glared. 'Izzy never touched that chick. If anybody tried to hit on anything, it was *her* trying to hit on Izzy when Vince wasn't around. Only Izzy didn't buy it. So that's what that's all about . . .'

Axl was referring to an incident that took place at the annual MTV awards for 1989 held in LA some weeks before. Izzy and Axl had just left the stage after jamming live for the cameras with Tom Petty when the itinerant Motley Crue singer appeared out of the backstage darkness and punched Izzy in the face.

'I hate to give Vince Neil or Motley Crue any credit like this, you know. But he's goin' around saying a bunch of crap and it's like, I just want to call him out on it. It's like, he's a liar and he's a wimp. And it's like, if he wants to do somethin' – any time, you know? At wherever. Name a place. Bring who you want. I don't care . . .'

He was obviously pretty worked up about it.

'I don't know. I'm pretty calm about it, actually,' he said, looking anything but. 'It's kind of like, just whenever you wanna do it, man. Let's just do it. I think it's be fun.' He bared his teeth. 'It's like, 'cos this way I can basically get away with it legally and everything, man. I can have a full-on brawl and get away with it.' His small freckled face brightened at the thought. 'I don't know, though, man, I don't know if I wanna hit the guy with that plastic face. It'll cave in . . .' He shucked it up.

Axl sat with his back to the balcony window, an undraped glass wall, the lights of the city twinkling behind his head like some vast dark garden of fireflies. I sat opposite him, an impressive art-deco glass coffee-table planted solidly between us.

'This is the third one I've had,' he remarked, running a hand lovingly across its surface.

What happened to the other two, I asked politely?

'I got pissed and smashed 'em,' he replied matter-of-factly. Oh . . .

Of course, Axl the life-threatening home-wrecker was an image the hyperactive Guns N' Roses frontman had never found hard to live up to. On stage he was a firebrand. And in interviews he was known to be equally volatile. He was articulate and he knew it. A smart-ass. Yet what drove him, he said, were the same simple desires he walked off the bus with when he first arrived in LA seven years ago. The simplest things still amused him; but the ugliest things were what enthralled him. He had a country hick's sense of humour shackled to a tough city kid's nous and, in the vernacular, he had one bad attitude.

'I've got this little psycho-ball. It's just the thing at times like this,' he said, his voice as deep as a well. 'Where did it go?' Then he found what he was looking for amongst the empty Coke cans, cigarette packets, magazines and ashtrays that littered the table – a small, apparently harmless rubber ball. He squeezed it and a terrible wheezing scream filled the room. Axl immediately cheered up. 'It's supposed to be for helping to relieve tension . . .' Another squeeze. Another long, nerve-jangling wail. 'I use it all the time . . . I had one like it and it was a fart-ball,' he explained. Then he launched into an improbable story about his friend, co-conspirator and songwriter, Wes Arkeen, getting drunk and causing ructions with the fart-ball at a Hollywood bar called the Mayflower.

'Wes gets all drunk. He was getting drunk every day. He got thrown out of the bar and cut off more times than anybody in history. And, like, all these actors, Nick Nolte and stuff, have partied there for years. So they've dealt with all this before but Wes would get cut off for breakfast, cut off for lunch, cut off for dinner and then talk 'em into opening the bar at three-thirty in the morning so they can make another drink, right?' He smiled like an indulgent mother. 'And it was gnarly, right? And so he's got this fart-ball, and he goes downstairs with it, you know, and he's all wasted. And he's beside this older couple and stuff and he, like, keeps doing this fart-ball' – he demonstrated for me again with the psycho-ball and another mad wail bit the air – 'and making, like, weird faces and fanning his rear end and stuff, like he just farted, like, "Oh . . . what was *that*?" And these people go, "You're disgusting!" and they move away.

'OK, so then I get this call from Sean Penn, his company or what-ever – these people that work for him – and he wants me to come see an advance screening of his new movie, *Casualties of War*. And if I want, you know, I can bring Wes. So Wes comes up and he's wasted.

So I throw him in the fuckin' shower, help him get dressed and we headed out of there down to the lobby. And there's this old couple there and this lady introduces herself and goes, "And this is Sean Penn's parents and they'll be going with you." I said, "Hi, my name's Axl and this is Wes . . ." And they were like, "Oh no! You're that guy in the bar!"' He laughed and looked me in the eye for the first time. 'It was Sean Penn's parents, you know . . . it was so great.

'Then we got in the back of this station-wagon, and there's these little fold-down seats and we're sitting on them. And, like, somebody pulled up in a car – we were trying to get out of there before these people arrived that were coming to my room – and suddenly there they were. And we were like, "Oh, fuck . . ." And then I went, "Oh, I'm sorry," and Sean Penn's dad turns round and goes, "Listen, goddamnit, don't ever fuckin' talk like that again, you understand me?" And then spins around and starts laughing because he just cussed me out.' He chuckled. 'I thought it was just great. Those guys were great . . .'

Talk of Wes, however, prompted a more recent and painful memory, as Axl recounted how Wes had had his nose broken in a fight in a bar over Christmas. 'He went down to a bar, or a liquor store, really drunk and some guy said something and got in Wes's face. Wes said something back and the guy just smashed a beer bottle in his nose.' He scrutinised the walls. 'That's fucking unreal, huh?' Axl sat there for a moment, skipping TV channels with the remote, gazing at several screens at once, all of them silent, like a scene from the *Welcome to the Jungle* video – minus the bouffant hairdo, a contemptuous smile on his face.

I mentioned the latest 'hot rumour' being quoted widely in the British gutter press, concerning the alleged reformation of the Sex Pistols, with Axl supposedly taking the place at the front previously occupied by Johnny Rotten (né Lydon).

Axl was dismissive. 'We just jammed with Steve Jones, that's all. He comes up to Slash's, we talk on the phone. It's like he's a friend of the family, you know? Slash is really into the guitar parts on the Steve Jones record. And I really like a lot of the songs. And we did the one Sex Pistols song together on it, "Did You No Wrong". You know, so we try and get up and jam with him whenever we can. I mean, I slept through his New Year's Eve gig and I was supposed to do three songs with him, man. But I hadn't slept in, like, three days and now it's like I feel really bad about it. I definitely owe him one.

'And the guy gets screwed over, man,' he continued, smiling dolefully. 'He did the Palace [Theatre, in Hollywood] and they put the curtain down when Slash and I were setting up at the side of the stage getting ready to do the encore, you know? They walked off stage, we were gonna walk right back on, and this guy shut the curtain and told the curtain guy to leave it 'cos he didn't want the show to continue! So we went down and I grabbed the guy – you know, I was with Steve Jones and stuff – and I grabbed the guy and he was like, "I don't like your hand on my shoulder." I was like, "I don't give a fuck what you like! Put the curtain up or I'm gonna go out there and start a riot!" But then they'd taken the drum-set down and once the mikes and the drum-set are down it's over, you know? So it was like . . . fucked.

'Then another time [at the Palace a few weeks before] we were supposed to do "Suffragette City" with Mick Ronson and Ian Hunter – Steve Jones and Slash and me. But then Steve decided he didn't wanna stick around, so me and Slash got up and did "White Light/White Heat" with Ian and Mick. I didn't even know the song and neither did Slash, we learned it really quick right before we walked on stage. I remember just following Ian around going ooh wooh, white light, la la . . . It was fuckin' great.'

Axl's face grew darker as his thoughts started to drift back towards Vince Neil. He didn't seriously believe Vince would take him up on his blunt offer and arrange to meet him and fight it out, did he?

'I've no idea what he will do,' he muttered sombrely. 'I mean, he could wait until I'm drunk in the Troubadour one night and get a phone call and come down and hit me with a beer bottle. But it's like, I don't care. Hit me with a beer bottle, dude! Do whatever you wanna do but I'm gonna take you out . . . I don't care what he does. Unless he sniper-shoots me – unless he gets me like that without me knowing it – I'm gonna take him with me.'

What if Vince were to apologise, though?

'That would be radical! Personally, I don't think he has the balls. I don't think he has the balls to admit he's been lying out of his ass. That would be great, though, if he did, and then I wouldn't have to be a dick from then on.'

I told Axl that I had heard David Bowie had apologised to him after the much-publicised fracas at a Guns N' Roses video-shoot some months before. The story goes that Axl had gotten pissed off with the ageing superstar after he appeared to be getting a little too well acquainted with Axl's girlfriend, Erin, during an unexpected visit to the set where the Gunners were then making the yet-to-see-the-light-of-day video for 'It's So Easy'. The upshot being that Axl reportedly aimed a few well-chosen punches Bowie's way before having him thrown off the set . . .

'Bowie and I had our differences,' he said coolly. 'And then we went out for dinner and talked and went to the China Club and stuff, you know, and when we left I was like, "I wanna thank you. You're the first person that's ever come up and said I'm sorry about the situation." You know, I didn't, like, try to take away any of his dignity or respect – like *Rolling Stone* saying I've no respect for the Godfather of Glam even though I wore make-up in this or that video and dah dah dah . . .

'It's like, when we opened for the Stones Mick Jagger and Eric Clapton cornered me, right? I go out there to do the soundcheck, and I'm sitting on this amp and all of a sudden they're both right there in front of me. And Jagger doesn't really talk a lot, right? He doesn't really talk at all, he's just real serious about everything. And all of a sudden he was like' – he assumed a theatrical Dick Van Dyke cockney – '"So you got in a fight with Bowie, didja?" You know, and I'm like . . . I told him the story real quick and him and Clapton are going off about Bowie in their own little world, talking about things from years of knowing each other. They were saying that when Bowie gets drunk he turns into the Devil from Bromley . . . I mean, I'm not even *in* this conversation. I'm just sitting there and every now and then they would ask me a couple more facts about what happened, and then they would go back to bitchin' like crazy about Bowie. I was just sitting there going, wow . . .

'But Bowie was really cool. We went to this restaurant and, like, it was just supposed to be Slash and me and Bowie and his girlfriend. Then I'm going and I bring an old friend of ours called Danny, who's an old roadie who's been through, like, crazy stories with cops and everything. We haven't been able to find Danny for two years. And Danny was like Dan the Man, he was a big part of our lives. But we couldn't find Danny. Well, I find Danny and another guy called Eric – two guys we haven't seen for a while that Slash and I used to hang with. So I bring them. Then Izzy shows up with Jimmy from Broken Homes, and we have this crowded table, right? And everybody's getting wasted on wine and stuff.

'Then Bowie comes around the table and he squats down next to me and starts talking. And all of a sudden somebody hit the table and my elbow, like, bumped his cheek, just real lightly. And he goes, "OH, FUCK!" and grabs his eye and jumps up, and the whole restaurant spins round . . . 'Cos they did not like me and Slash being in the restaurant anyway, OK? This doesn't usually happen any more but this place it happened in 'cos they were all, you know, all quiet, with an art gallery showing on the walls and all this stuff.

'And the people running the restaurant don't know who . . . It's not like they don't know who I am, but they don't give a flying fuck. They don't know it's Slash and Axl, they just see us coming in in leather jackets and stuff and they're freaking, right?

'So there's a whole table and we're all getting loud and stuff. But Bowie's there so they've got to let this go on, they don't know what else to do, right? It was great. So Bowie jumps up and goes, "OH FUCK!" and the whole place spins around, and the ladies and stuff are hiding behind their fuckin' menus. Then he goes, "Just kidding! Just fucking kidding!" It was great, it was great . . .' More hoarse laughter.

'We went to the China Club and stuff and he, like, had me do photos with him. He was like, "I don't know if you wanna do this, but . . ." He was really cool. We started talking about the business and I never met anybody so cool and so into it and so whacked out and so sick in my life. I looked over at Slash and I went, "Man, we're in fuckin' deep trouble." He goes, "Why?" And I go, "'Cos I got a lot in common with this guy. I mean, I'm pretty sick but this guy's just fuckin' ill!" And Bowie's sittin' there laughing . . . Then he starts talking about, "One side of me is experimental, and one side of me wants to make something that people get into. And I DON'T KNOW FUCKING WHY! WHY AM I LIKE THIS!?" And I'm, like, thinking to myself, I've got twenty more years of . . . *that* to look forward to? I'm already like this! Twenty more years? It was heavy, man . . .'

Axl began to reflect on the year just past. He talked plaintively of 'wasting time just trying to get it together', citing the aborted trip to Chicago the previous summer as a particularly grisly example. 'We got into these fights in Chicago. I was, like, just into fuckin' everybody's music – getting into Slash's stuff, getting into Duff's stuff. Our timing schedules were all weird and we kept showing up at different times. But when I would show up, I'm like, OK, let's do this, let's do that, let's do this one of yours, Slash. OK, now let's go to this one, and Steven needs to do this . . . And then they decided I was a dictator, right? I'm a total dictator and I'm a completely selfish dick.' He looked bemused. 'I was like, fuck, man . . . And we were on a roll, man! You know, we were cranking.

'Slash is like, "We're not gettin' nothin' done." I was like, "What do you mean? We just put down six parts of new songs, you know, we've just got all this stuff done in, like, a couple weeks!" He was like, "Yeah, but I've been sitting here a month on my ass . . ." This was while I was driving across country in my truck, you know. Like, yeah, let's party! Shoot guns!' Another deep chuckle.

They say that every successful band needs a dictator in the line-up, just to kick people's backsides occasionally and keep things in motion. Was that one of the roles Axl saw himself fulfilling in Guns N' Roses – the dictator of the band?

'Listen, after working with Jagger it was like, don't ever call me a dictator again, man.' He smiled wanly. 'You can go and work for the Stones and you'll learn the hard way . . .'

Did Axl get to spend any time with Jagger at all other than that one conversation with Clapton about Bowie?

'I didn't really hang out with him.' He shook his head and lit a cigarette. 'That guy walks off stage and goes and does paperwork. He says' – Axl switched back to the Dick Van Dyke cockney – '"Excuse me, I've got to do paperwork . . ."'

Checking the gate receipts?

'Everything! Every fuckin' thing. That guy is involved in every little aspect, you know, from what the background singers are getting paid to how much we're paying for this part of the PA. He is on top of all of it. It's him and his lawyer, OK? And a couple of guys that he hangs with, you know, part of the entourage. But basically, it's all him . . .'

And as for the other Glimmer Twin, Axl said he only got to meet Keith Richards once or twice, and then only briefly.

'We talked but I just kind of like watched the guy. Basically, I told him I gotta go shopping, 'cos he has the coolest fur coats and shit in the world, and he just loved that. He laughed pretty hard at that one. And I asked him about Billy Idol saying he got pissed off over "Rebel Yell". Keith goes, "Stole it off my fuckin' night-table, he did!" I thought that was great . . .'

Meeting former teenhood heroes, however, could be a nerve-racking affair, said Axl, recalling a somewhat strained recent meeting with Who bass player John Entwhistle. 'It's like, I had always read this rumour, like in *Keyboard Player* magazine and stuff, that for the keyboard part of "Baba O'Reilly" Townshend went and got brain-waves, right? Then programmed it through a computer and copied them for the keyboard part,' he explained, ignoring the face I was pulling. 'So I asked Entwhistle, and Entwhistle's, like, annihilated out of his mind and he's in his own little world anyway, and he goes, "Brainwaves? What fuckin' brainwaves? Townsend ain't got no goddamn brainwaves!"' he smiled. 'You know, but yet Townsend's a genius and he knows it but it was just out of humour, you know? It was like a band camaraderie thing, you know, jiving each other. I thought it was cool . . .

'Then I asked him about the time he was supposed to have shot up all his gold records, and he said, "I'll let you in on a secret, mate. Those were Connie Francis' records, I fuckin' stole 'em! I aint gonna shoot my *own* goddamn gold records, am I?" I was like, wow, OK, I've had enough of this guy, I can't deal with it any more. He's blowing my mind!' More throaty chuckling. "'Cos he was fuckin' lit and ready to go, man. Still standing all stiff and straight and ready to fuckin' do whatever . . .'

Axl took another swig from his Coke can and began to talk again about his experiences working with the Rolling Stones. 'Ron Wood made this thing go back together and worked on putting it back together, right? OK, but Mick makes it happen. With the looseness that those guys have and the amount of people around them you need somebody being the general, you know? And he does it. He has to do it. 'Cos the frontman . . . you don't plan on that job. You don't want that job. You don't want to be that guy to the guys in your band that you hang with and you look up to. But somebody's got to do it. And the guitar player can't do it because he is not the guy who . . . he can go back, hang his hair down in his face and stand back by the amps and get into his guitar part.

'The frontman has to be communicating with eye-contact and hand movements and moving around in the crowd, and directing his energy to that entire audience. Like someone goes, "You're gonna have a huge arena tour next year, dude." And I go, "I know, but that's the problem, 'cos I can work a stadium now!" And I can. I can work a fuckin' stadium, and that's what I wanna do, you know?' His eyes shone. Then the flame died. 'So it won't be the same rush working in an arena as working a stadium. I mean, when we did the Stones show I *ran* that track, and that was a blast! I was like, I've always wanted to fuckin' do this! That was a blast . . .'

What about his little 'retirement' speech: was Axl actually serious, or was he, as his critics had claimed at the time, merely touting for more controversial headlines for himself and his band?

'No.' He was adamant. 'That was definite and that was serious. I mean, I offered to go completely broke and back on the streets, 'cos it would have cost, like, an estimated $1.5 million to cancel the shows, OK? That means Axl's broke, OK? Except what I've got tied up in Guns N' Roses' interests or whatever. But I didn't want to do that because I wouldn't want the band to have to pay for me cancelling the shows. I don't want Duff to lose his house 'cos Axl cancelled the shows. I couldn't live with that. But at the same time I'm not gonna be a part of watching them kill each other, just killing themselves off. It's like, it came down to like, we tried every other angle of getting our shit back together and in the end it had to be done live. You know, everybody else was pissed at me but afterwards Slash's mom came and shook my hand and so did his brother.'

But had it worked, though? Had the culprits – Slash, Izzy and Steven – actually done the right thing and cleaned up their acts?

He nodded his head vigorously. 'It way worked, man! 'Cos Slash is fuckin' on like a motherfucker right now. And the songs are coming together, they're coming together real heavy. And I've written all these ballads, right? But Slash has written all these really heavy crunch rockers . . .'

Had it largely been the drugs, then, that had kept Guns N' Roses out of the recording studio these past twelve months?

'Partly,' Axl acknowledged. 'But another reason things have been so hard in a way is this. The first album was basically written off Axl coming up with maybe one line and maybe a melody for that line or how I want to present that line, how I'm gonna say it or yell it or whatever, OK? And then we'd build a song around it. Or someone came up with one line, OK?

'On this, Izzy's brought in eight songs – at least. Slash has brought in an album, I've brought in an album. And Duff knows everybody's material, OK? Duff brought in one song. He said all his in one song. It's called "Why Do You Look at Me When You Hate Me?" And it's just bad-assed. And I wrote a bunch of words to that, but Duff brought in the song. And it's like, he knows everybody's songs and when anybody else has been too wasted or somethin', no matter how wasted Duff is he's *on* in rehearsal and holds everything together with the strong bass. No matter how fucked everybody else is.

'So now it's got to a point where . . . See, we never had Izzy's material in on any of this before. Except for that one song written before the first album ["Patience"] – we never had any of Izzy's material. But Izzy's songs have this, like, wry sense of humour, man, you know?

'You know, and the rhythm reminds me of something like "Cherokee People" or whatever, by Paul Revere and the Raiders, man. It's like, really weird but it's like, rocked out. It's really weird . . .'

117

The phone rang and I turned off the tape for a moment while Axl stooped to answer it – it was buried beneath a pile of cushions at his feet. I was anxious to move the conversation on to the barbed subject of the controversy that still raged over the lyrics to 'One in a Million'. I had heard Slash and Duff loyally defend the song countless times, now I wanted to know what Axl's views were. But he beat me to it.

'One thing I could talk about I haven't talked about yet,' he said when he got off the phone. 'We've had a lot of people that were behind the band, different magazines and this and that. And some of the magazines you're into, some of them maybe you're not so into. But you do, like, appreciate the help you got from the magazines, OK? Now we've only done certain interviews recently – or I have. And people have been offended and this and that. So then, like, what's happened is a lot of them have gone, OK, well this guy that works for my magazine hates Guns N' Roses, write a piece on "One in a Million"! Because someone was pissed off, right?'

All right, I said carefully, but didn't Axl think certain writers and communicators might have their own reasons for throwing their hands up in rage? That the concern, the outrage might after all be sincere?

'But that's not . . .' He paused. ' "One in a Million", there's a lot of things to think about and talk about in that, you know? But, like, I don't think people understand some of the press's motivations for going after the song in the ways they have.'

Axl admitted he hadn't anticipated the size and the scale of the negative reaction the song would provoke. 'We weren't really prepared for what happened. I used a word, it's part of the English language whether it's a good word or not. It's a derogatory word, it's a negative word. It's not meant to the entire black race, but it was directed towards black people in those situations,' he declared guardedly. 'I was robbed, I was ripped off, you know? I had my life threatened, OK? And it's like, I described it in one word. And I wanted to see the effect of a racial joke. I wanted to see the effect that would have on the world. Slash was into it.

'You know, we've been nice. We haven't talked about . . . We haven't tried to analyse this and think maybe we should be more like this and that. It wasn't contrived so much as we were trying to grow with it, you know, and grow with our thoughts. Now after getting beat up over it in the press we're like, hey, fuck you! We fuckin' said something. Now a black person on Oprah Winfrey who goes, "They're putting down black people!" is going to fuckin' take one of these guys at the bus stop home and feed him and take care of him and let him baby-sit their kids?' he asked disdainfully. 'They ain't gonna be *near* the guy, OK?

'And it's like, I don't think a black person is a nigger. I don't care. I'm like, they're whatever, you know? I consider myself, like, green and from another planet or something, you know? I never felt I fairly fit into any group, so to speak. But it's like . . . a black person has this three hundred years of whatever on his shoulder. I don't got nothin' to do with that! It bores me, too.'

What about what Vernon Reid had had to say about it, though, on stage at the Coliseum the night of the first Stones show?

He smiled the indulgent-mother smile again. 'It's like, Vernon Reid was talking about how people make racial jokes, but that it was kind of sad. Because you'll laugh but then, after all, when you think about it, it is sad. But humour and comedy, you know, everybody makes fun of everybody and everything. It's kind of like you go, well, I can't find a way to be happy, maybe I can find something to laugh at for a moment and take my mind off things, you know? Whether I mean it or not. Just somethin' to laugh at. You know, you could watch a movie about someone blowing the crap out of these people and you could be the most anti-violent person in the world. But yet get off on this movie – "Yeah, he deserved it!" you know? The bad guy got shot . . . It's like a double-edged sword a lot of times.'

Was that all 'One in a Million' was, then: a joke? Just more egg on somebody else's face?

'Something I've noticed that's really weird about "One in a Million" is the whole song coming together took me by surprise. I mean, yeah, I wrote the song as a joke. Wes just got robbed by two black guys on Christmas night a few years back. He went out to play guitar on Hollywood Boulevard in front of a bank at, like, Highland and Holly-wood. You know, he's standing there playing and he gets robbed at knife-point for seventy-eight cents.' His voice didn't sound incredulous so much as comically resigned. Like the black sheep younger brother Woody Allen never talked about.

'A couple of days later we're all sittin' around, we're watching TV, there's Duff and me and Wes and a couple of others. And we're all bummed out, hungover and this and that. And I'm sittin' there pissed off with no money, no job, feeling guilty for being at Wes's house, you know, sucking up oxygen and stuff . . . And I got hold of this guitar – and I can only play, like, the top two strings, right? But I'd been fuckin' around with this little riff for a while, little by little. It was the only thing I could play on the guitar.

'So all of a sudden I wanted to write some words as a joke, right?

We'd just watched Sam Kinnison or somethin' on the video, you know, so I was gonna make my jokes, too. So I started writing this thing. And when I said *"Police and niggers . . ."* that was to fuck with Wes's head. 'Cos he couldn't believe I would write that, right? And it came out like that, OK? Later on, the chorus came about because I was getting, like, really far away, like "Rocket Man" Elton John, you know, like in my head. Gettin' really far away from all my friends and family in Indiana . . . I realised those people have no concept of who I am any more, even the ones I was close to.' He lingered over his cigarette.

'Since then I've flown people out here, had 'em hang out here. I've paid for everything.' He perked up, flying off on another tangent. 'But there was no joy in it for them. I was smashing shit, goin' fuckin' nuts. And yet trying to work. And they were going, "Man, I don't wanna be a rocker any more if you go through this."' The thin scarecrow shoulders shook with mirth.

'But at the same time, you know, I brought 'em out and we just hung out for a couple months, wrote songs together, you know, had serious talks. It was almost like being on acid, 'cos it would just get to serious talks about the family and life and stuff. And we'd get really heavy and get to know each other all over again. Just trying to fuckin' replace eight years of knowing each other every single day, you know, and now all of a sudden I'm in this new world . . .

'Back there I was a street kid with a skateboard and no money who talked about being in a rock band. And now all of a sudden I'm here, you know? And they're kind of amused, freaked-out and all kinds of stuff by their friends putting up Axl posters, and it's just weird to them. And this business and all that, like they ask, why don't I call? It's like, well come out here and watch how many times my phone rings. It doesn't ring that much tonight because nobody thinks I'm here . . .' He paused, trying to remember where he was.

'So anyway, all of a sudden I came up with this chorus . . . Everybody was into dope then and those analogies are great in rock songs. Aerosmith done proved that on their old stuff, and the Stones. And drug analogies, like, the language is always the hippest language, you know? A lot of hip-hop, even the stuff that's like anti-drugs, a lot of the terms and stuff come off of some drug street rap. 'Cos they're always on top of stuff, those guys. They gotta change their language all the time so people don't know what they're saying so they can, you know, keep dealing. Plus they're trying to be the hippest, coolest, baddest thing out there.

'And " you're one in a million..." someone said that to me real sarcastically. It wasn't like an ego thing, oh I'm one in a million, you know? Originally it was kinda like someone went, "Yeah, you're just fuckin' one in a million, aren't ya?" And it stuck with me, you know? So I put that chorus together and then it fit this other thing, I couldn't figure out why. Yet the song was done as a joke, and then there was this heavy chorus...'

If it was all such a joke, I interjected, how come nobody seemed to be laughing?

'Well,' he continued unabashed, 'we got in the studio and I realised I didn't have good enough timing on the guitar. I'd never played this song except for once every couple of months, you know, as a joke at a party or somethin'. And Duff plays it much more aggressively. Slash made it too tight and concise. I wanted it a bit rawer, because I was into some old Stones stuff and I liked this raw edge. I mean, our music is different and it's '89, it's not sixty-something or early seventies. But yet I wanted that feel. And then Izzy comes up with this electric guitar thing. I was pushing him to come up with a cool tone and all of a sudden he's coming up with this aggressive thing. It just *happened*.

'So suddenly it didn't work to sing the whole song in a low funny voice any more . . . ' He began to sing . It just didn't work, it didn't fit and it didn't sound right. And the guitar parts they played were so cool I had to sing it like HURRHHH! So it sounds like I'm totally into this. But no, this is just one point of view out of hundreds that I have on the situation. When I meet a black person I deal with each situation differently. Like I deal with it with every person I meet. It doesn't matter.'

Though his name had been mercilessly kicked around in every corner of the media for the ill-chosen words to 'One in a Million', Axl said he had not actually suffered any real abuse personally from any of the ordinary black people he had encountered on his travels. Quite the opposite, in fact, he assured me.

'Actually, I meet a lot of black people that come up and just wanna talk about it and discuss it with me because they find it interesting. Like, a black chick came up to me when we were in Chicago and goes, "You know, I hated you 'cos of 'One in a Million'." I'm standing at a bar and I'm like, "Oh, great, another one. Can I have another drink please?" Then she goes, "But I ride the subway," and all of a sudden she got real serious. She goes, "And I looked around one day and I know what you're talking about. So you're all right." And I've got a lot of that . . .'

What about from other musicians, though? Living Colour's Vernon Reid, for example, certainly had plenty to say on the subject in public. What about in private?

'It's like, I had this big heavy conversation with [black LA rappers] Ice T and Ezee E. Ice T sent a letter, wanting to work with me on "Welcome to the Jungle" if I ever did it as a rap thing. And I got the word to Ezee E that I'm interested in having him be a part of it too, if we ever do it. I mean, don't think it'll be on this record now, there's already too much material. But we ended up having this big heavy conversation about "One in a Million", and they could see where I was coming from. And those guys know more about that shit than most . . .'

'We haven't done a lot of press things lately, not so much out of, like, Well, fuck you guys, we don't need you, or this and that, you know? It's just been kind of like . . . I mean, we want Guns N' Roses to be huge and stuff and we're glad when we get offered different interviews and all this stuff. But at the same time, you know, we get a bit sick of it, too. Seeing our faces all over the place.

'And at the same time, you don't want so much over-exposure and so you kind of like go, OK, I'm gonna do *one* piece. OK, which magazine am I gonna do that in? What audience do I want to hit with what I'm gonna say, you know? Like, how am I going to approach this interview? It's like, if I'm doing a *Rolling Stone* interview, it's not so much catering to the audience, it's like I'm just gonna use a different facet of my personality, 'cos I figure I'm talking to different people. With *Rolling Stone* you're talking to U2 fans, REM, you know, and different crowds, OK, than you're talking to in *RIP* . . . So maybe what I want to say needs to be said that way. So you do one interview rather than, like, trying to keep on top of *Metal Edge, Metallix, Blast*, you know, and all the Japanese magazines – *Burn, Music Life* and all the others. 'Cos it's like, we've had to focus in on trying to get our lives together to deal with this, you know? And we're just now getting some things under control.

''Cos once we start touring and we get a touring budget and the cash comes in from touring and stuff like that our lifestyle's gonna completely change all over again.' He shook his head slowly. ''Cos it's all still new to us, it's not something we've been around forever.'

And so, inevitably and with something approaching reluctance, but you never know, Axl returned to the subject of the next Guns N' Roses album . . .

'There's, like, thirty-seven songs, and I know by the end of the record there'll be forty-two to forty-five and I want thirty of them down.'

It was definitely going to be a double album then?

'Well, a double record but a single 76-minute CD. OK? Then I want five B-sides – people never listen to B-sides that much – and that will be the backside of another EP. You know, we'll say it's B-sides. Plus, there should be four extra songs for an EP, *if* we pull this off, OK? So that's the next record. And then there's the live record from the tour . . . If we can pull this thing off, if we do this right, it'll be five years before we have to make another album.' Though he smiled as he said this it was obvious it wasn't the first time this thought had occurred to Axl.

'Sure. And we can have five years to . . . It's not so much like five years to sit on our asses. It's like, five years to figure out what we're gonna say next, you know? After the crowd and the people figure out how they're gonna react to this album, and then the mental changes we will go through . . .'

What kind of direction did Axl see the band taking on this next album? Did he plan to expand on his usual themes somewhat, or was he going to stick to the same sleazy half-world undercurrents of the first album for inspiration?

'This record will have seen us grown a lot,' he stated confidently. 'There'll be some childish, you know, arrogant, male, false bravado crap on there, too. But there'll also be some really heavy, serious stuff.'

Nevertheless, by the time the new album – I was tempted to add 'if the new album' – eventually saw the light of day, it would be such a ridiculously long time since the release of *Appetite*, and what with everything that will have gone down in between, Axl admitted he

123

sensed the rumblings of the inevitable backlash already beginning to build.

'But it doesn't fuckin' matter,' he asserted. 'This doesn't matter, man. This is too *late* . . . If we record this album the way we wanna record this album, it could bomb, but five years from now there'll be a lot of kids into it in Hollywood. Ten years from now it'll be an underground thing like early Aerosmith and Hanoi Rocks. Because the material has strong enough lyrical content and strong enough guitar parts, you'll have no choice. It'll permeate into people's brains one way or another,' he predicted. 'It's like, if the album doesn't fuckin' sell and be successful, some band ten years from now is gonna write a record and we're gonna be one of their main influences. And so the message is still gonna get through – whatever we're trying to say and the things we're trying to say, it's always gonna get through. Not so much like, our message is the way.' He looked thoughtful. 'But there's an audience for what we're saying that's going through the same things we are. And in a way, we *are* leading. Not like we're leading the whole rock 'n' roll world, but . . .'

But what? To my mind, Guns N' Roses undeniably led the way – both artistically and commercially – in terms of what was, and just as importantly what *wasn't* happening in modern rock music.

Axl said he was conscious of that but still didn't feel entirely comfortable in a role he insisted had largely been foisted upon him. 'It's been . . . shown to me in a lot of ways,' he said, toying with the psycho-ball again. 'I didn't want to accept the responsibility really, even though I was trying, but I still was reluctant to the idea. Now I'm kind of into it. Because it's like, you have a choice, man. You can grow or die, you know? And it's like, that's what we have to do. We have to do it. We have to grow. You know, we can't do the same sludge. I can't play sludge, man, for fuckin' twenty years!'

I rolled the conversation on: 1989 seemed to have been a peculiar year for the band.

'Yeah, but if you look at it, it's not peculiar at all. Because number one, we had to find a whole new way of working together, because everybody got *successful*.' He leaned heavily on the last word. 'OK? And everybody's had a dream that when they got successful they could do what they want. And so that ends up with Slash bringing in eight songs. It's never been done before, Slash bringing in a song first and me writing words to it. I've done it twice with him before and we didn't use either of those songs. Out of Slash's choice. Now he's got eight of them that I gotta write words to and they're bad-assed songs! Meantime, I was working on, like, writing these ballads that I feel have really rich tapestries and stuff, and making sure each note in effect is right.

''Cos I also write with a lot of . . . whether I'm using a lot of instrumentation and stuff, I'll still write with minimalism, right? But it has to be the right note and it has to be held in the right way and it has to have the right effect, you know?'

I said I never knew that Axl was such a perfectionist . . .

'Sure. But what people don't understand is that there was a perfectionist attitude to *Appetite For Destruction*. I mean, there was a definite plan to that. We could have made it all smooth and polished. We went and did test tracks with other producers and it came out smooth and polished – with Spencer Proffer. And Geffen Records said it was *too* fuckin' radio. That's why we went with Mike Clink. We went for a raw sound, because it just didn't gel having it too tight and concise. We knew this. We knew the way we are on stage and the only way to capture that on the record is to make it somewhat live. Doing the bass, the drums and the rhythm guitar at the same time. Getting the best track, having it a bit faster than you play it live, OK, so that brings some energy into it. Adding lots of vocal parts and overdubs with the guitars, adding more music to capture . . .' He looked up at me hopefully but I didn't know the right words either.

''Cos Guns N' Roses on stage, man, can be, like, out to lunch. Visually, we're all over the place and stuff and you don't know what to expect. But how do you get that on a record? But somehow you have to do that. So there's a lot more that's needed on a record. That's why recording is my favourite thing, because it's like painting a picture. You start out with a shadow, or an idea, and you come up with something that's a shadow of that. You might like it better. It's still not exactly what you pictured in your head, though.

'And then you add all these things and you come up with something you didn't even expect . . . Slash will do, like, one slow little guitar fill that adds a whole different mood that you didn't expect. That's what I love. All of a sudden it's like you're doing a painting and then you go away and you come back and it's different. You use the brush this way and allow a little shading to come in and you go, "Wow, I got a whole different effect on this that's even heavier than what I pictured. I don't know quite what I'm onto but I'm on it," you know?

'"Paradise City", man,' he continued, eyes ablaze now. 'That's like, I came up with two of those first vocals – there's five parts there – I came up with two and they sounded really weird. Then I said, look, I got an idea. I put two of these vocal things together, and it was the two

125

weirdest ones, the two most obtuse ones. 'And Clink's like, "I don't know about that, man . . ." I'm like, "I don't know either, why don't we just sleep on it?" So we go home and the next day I call him up and now I'm like, "I don't know about this." But he goes, 'No, I think it's cool!" So now he was the other way . . . So then we put three more vocal parts on it and then it fit. But the point is, that wasn't how we had it planned. We don't really know how it happened.'

Axl confided that ultimately he much preferred the whole business of recording to its wilder twin sister, touring. 'If I'm psyched for the gig, great. Nine times out of ten, though, before the gig I'll always not wanna do the fuckin' show and hate it. I mean, I love it when I'm psyched, you know, let's go! But most of the time I'm, like, mad about something, something's fuckin' going wrong . . . I'm nervous. I'm like, "I'm not playing for these fuckin' people!"'

Which people? The audience?

'Not the crowd so much. It's like, I'm not playing for whoever's putting on the show, or like that. We have a lot of good relationships with promoters and stuff, so I don't want that to be taken as the main example,' he added cautiously. 'But you know, situations are always different before a show. Something always fuckin' happens. Something *always* happens. And I react like a motherfucker to it. I don't like this pot-smoking mentality.' He sucked in his cheeks. 'I feel like Lenny Kravitz . . . Like, peace and love, motherfucker, or you're gonna die! I'm gonna kick your ass if you fuck with my garden, you know? I like that attitude more.'

Had the overwhelming fame thrust upon him and his cohorts so suddenly and so voraciously bolstered that attitude, though?

'What do you mean?' he looked at me suspiciously.

You know, forced you to be larger than life, I prodded. Obnoxious because he knew there would always be somebody there to take care of it?

A long pause. 'No.' He was sure. 'I've always been that way,' he told me, eyes narrowed. 'But now I'm in a position to just be myself more. And the thing is people allow me to do it whether they like it or not, you know?'

Did he feel he took advantage of that situation, though? To use the heights to which the public had elevated Guns N' Roses to shit on those he despised below?

Another long pause. 'No,' he eventually decided. 'No, usually I'm just an emotionally unbalanced person.' He tittered. 'Maybe it's chemical, I don't know. 'Cos maybe emotions have something to do with chemicals in your brain, or whatever. So then it's a chemical imbalance . . . And it's like, I'm usually an emotional wreck before a show anyway, because of something else that's going on in my life or whatever. I mean, something weird will happen in my family. Like, I finally found William Rose, OK? He was murdered in '84 and buried in seven miles of strip-mining in Illinois. I found that out, like, two days before a show and I was whacked, right? It was fuckin' gnarly . . .'

Axl wasn't so much upset by the news – not to mention the manner – of his natural father's death, he said, as he was disappointed not to have made the old man's acquaintance. 'I was trying to uncover this mystery since I was a little kid, you know? 'Cos as a kid I was always told that it was the Devil that made me know what the inside of a house looked like that I supposedly never lived in. But I *knew* I did. I knew I'd lived in this house when I was a little kid. Weird things like that happen . . . So I've been trying to track down this William Rose guy. Not like, I love this guy, he's my father. I just wanted to know about my heritage and what my hereditary traits might be. You know, am I gonna have an elbow that bugs the shit out of me in, like, three or four years. Is that a hereditary trait or what? I wanted to know.'

Axl had said his father was murdered. I asked gingerly if he knew exactly how his father had met his ugly demise?

'No. But it was probably, like, at close range, man,' he deadpanned. 'Wonderful family, man. Just wonderful . . .' He looked pensive for a moment. Then the cloud moved from his face. 'We're looking for Jeff Lynne,' he announced suddenly.

I was confused. Jeff Lynne? Electric Light Orchestra and Travelling Wilburys Jeff Lynne? I enquired, somewhat taken aback.

'Yeah,' he drawled, pleased by my surprise. 'I want him to work on "November Rain", and there's, like, three or four possible other songs that if that works out I'd like to use him on . . .'

For string arrangements, I hazarded a guess?

'Yeah. This record will be produced by Guns N' Roses and Mike Clink, OK? But I might be using synthesizer – but I'm gonna *say* I'm using synthesizer and what I programmed. It's not gonna be like, "Oh, you know, we do all our shows live," and then it's on tape. That's not the thing. I just want to . . . you know, jump into today. I have never had the money to do it before. And I thought maybe someone like Jeff Lynne could help.'

Mention of 'November Rain', already being touted by those supposedly in the know as one of the major highlights of the next Guns N' Roses album, reminded me of something Axl had been quoted as saying in *Rolling Stone*, to the effect that if 'November Rain' wasn't recorded to his complete satisfaction he would quit the music business.

'That was then.' He bowed his head. 'At that time it was the most important song to me.'

Did he still stick by his threat to leave the music business if it wasn't recorded properly, though?

'Yeah. That's the fuckin' truth. That's the fuckin' truth, all right. But the worst part of that is if, like, you're gonna look at it in a negative way, man, is I got four of those motherfuckers now, that I don't know *how* I wrote. And I like 'em *better* than "November Rain", and I'll crush that motherfuckin' song . . . And it's like, now I've got four of them that I gotta do and they're all big songs. We play 'em and we get chills and go "How did we do that? Let's go have a drink!"

'It happens all the time. We'll fuckin' write a whole song, we'll write the whole goddamned song out, the music, the words, this and that, the melodies, everything. We'll play the song, we'll learn it, we'll get it all completely down and then all of a sudden we'll go, "But what if we do this?" Like, uhhhh . . .' he grimaced, throwing up his hands in mock despair. 'And I did that in another way. I came in with this heavy piano part . . . It's like, real big. And it fits this blues-ish gospel thing that was supposed to be a blues-rocker, like "Buy Me a Chevrolet" by Foghat or somethin'. Now it's turned into this thing like "Take Another Piece of My Heart" [by Janis Joplin] or somethin'. We're like, how did we do this? We don't know but we'll just do it. And there's, like, *four* of those. . .'

I was still mulling over the giddy prospect of Jeff Lynne working on the next Guns N' Roses album. Why him? Was Axl a closet ELO freak, then?

'Oh yeah, I'm an old ELO fanatic!' he enthused, hands slicing the air like machettes. 'I love old ELO . . . *Out of the Blue*, that period. I went to see 'em play when I was kid and shit like that. I mean, I respect Jeff Lynne for being Jeff Lynne, but *Out of the Blue* is an awesome album . . .'

I was still baffled. What qualities did Jeff Lynne embody for Axl that he admired so much?

'Well, one: he's got stamina. Two: he's used to working with a lot of material. Three: he's used to working with all kinds of instrumentation. Four: he's used to working with all kinds of different styles of music. Five: he wrote all his own material. Six: he produced it.' He became wide-eyed for a moment. 'That's a lot of concentration and a lot of energy needed. Hopefully, I would like, if he's available, to have him. He's the best. I don't know if we can get him or not, but I'd like to try.'

And if they could find Jeff Lynne and actually get him to agree to work on the album – an unlikely outcome in the cold light of day – Axl would like him involved only for certain tracks?

'That's what we'd like to start with. I mean, who knows? Maybe him and Clink will hit it off just great and everybody'll be into it. Then great, welcome to it, you know?'

I remarked that Axl's tastes in music were obviously more far-reaching than one would anticipate from the average 'Heavy Metal' singer. 'I sure fuckin' hope so.' He smiled wryly. As a little game, I asked him to pick three tracks from his youth that, for whatever reason, best summed up his musical tastes, maybe even helped form them.

He thought about it for a moment then decided to oblige. The first track he picked was 'D'Ya Maker'; a rare Led Zeppelin hit single from their 1973 *Houses of the Holy* album. Axl admitted he'd never actually known what the correct pronunciation of the song was until I informed him that it was a play on the word 'Jamaica', the song itself having a strong reggae-feel – if not quite the beat.

'When I was in grade school I used to write down the names of, like, all the novelty songs. Like "Spiders and Snakes" [by Terry Jacks] and stuff like that. Then I heard "D'Ya Maker" and I made fun of it like crazy. I was telling everybody about this weird song I'd heard on the radio. So I'm laughing at it and this and that, but by recess in the afternoon I'm sitting in the corner with my pocket radio and I just had to hear that song again. I mean, I *had* to hear it. That was, like, the first case of "I have to hear that song". I had it going through my head and I had to hear it. And that got me into hard rock.'

Being then a student of classical piano, the first thing Axl did, he recalled, was try to learn how to play 'D'Ya Maker' on the family piano. An idea that caused a good deal of consternation in the household. 'I remember getting knocked right off the piano bench by my dad. 'Cos I had learnt it on the piano. I would play and then I would do the drum-break on the top and just beat the shit out of the piano. Then get knocked right off. Biff!' He smirked.

Axl was 'nine or ten' the first time he heard 'D'Ya Maker'. It was the first time he had heard of Led Zeppelin. 'I heard that and then I was hooked. After that I was Led Zeppelin all the way. That song just blew my mind. I thought, how does he write like this? How does he *feel* like this? I mean, 'cos everything around me was, like, religious and strict. Even though we were in a city we went to a country church and stuff. I mean, the language was so much different. There was no, whoah, cool vibe and stuff like in that Zeppelin song. It was like, how did he *think* like that, you know?'

129

For his second choice, Axl chose 'Benny and the Jets' from the 1973 Elton John double album, *Goodbye Yellow Brick Road*. I raised my eyebrows over that one. Though I shouldn't have. Axl once told me he was great admirer of Elton John's lyricist, Bernie Taupin. He'd even said he would like to interview Taupin about his lyrics for a magazine. So far, however, there had been no takers. Taupin, for his part, when asked for his opinion of the young Guns N' Roses singer's work, graciously replied that he was 'an admirer' and that he was particularly enamoured of the lyrics to 'Sweet Child o' Mine'.

'Elton John is the baddest! There's nobody badder when it comes to attacking the piano and using it in a rock sense. I mean, you're gonna tell me that "Saturday Night's Alright For Fighting" or "Grow Some Funk of Your Own", or like, "Ballad of a Well-known Gun" or "Somebody Saved My Life Tonight" and things like that ain't heavy songs? There's no way!' he crowed. 'Those guys wrote seven No. 1 albums in the U.S. from, like, '72 to '75 – in *three years*! Bernie Taupin was twenty-five years old, writing off the top of his head, writing albums in two hours! And the guy's vocabulary and education . . .' He shook his head in guileless awe.

'It was so amazing they decided to go rock 'n' roll rather than go classical or whatever. And they blended all these different styles. Amazing . . . And "Benny and the Jets",' he picked up the thread again, 'with the ambience and the sound and the way it's recorded, made me want the stage. That's the song that made me want the stage, 'cos it made me think about a concert and being on a stage and the way it would sound in a room. Things miked out and this and that . . . Plus, it just reminded me of the Glam scene that was going on around America, and the clubs that I would read about in the old *Creem* magazine and stuff like that.

'It's amazing. Elton John's singing is amazing and that piano solo can't be touched. It's an amazing record . . . Then when I got the piano book and was trying to learn the song, I discovered the guy's playing ten fingers of the weirdest chords in the world you know? It's like, what made him think to hit *this* combination of five notes – that makes the initial bomp-bomp-bomp? It's not just, like, a major note, it's all these weird combinations. He just pulls stuff off that nobody else does . . .'

Would he consider Elton John's music a major influence on his own songwriting style then?

'Sure,' he nodded approvingly. 'I've played piano in a style influenced by Elton John and Billy Joel. But it's minimalistic, you know? I know what I can and what I can't do, so I aim it real carefully. But it's

130

basically influenced off Elton John's attack. And his singing is amazing. If you want to learn how to sing all different styles, try singing like Elton John. Anything from the blues on. Anything.'

What about his post-eighties output, though?

'I don't know,' Axl wavered. But he was gentlemanly about it.

'His newer stuff to me is for an older audience. But, you know, they're older people now. But their younger stuff is still amazing, and it amazes me that radio in America doesn't give Elton John the space that they give Led Zeppelin, the Beatles and the Stones. You know, you don't have the Elton John Hour, yet you can have 400,000 people going to Central Park to see Elton John, and you're gonna have sold-out tours all over the country. I don't understand it.' And he looked like he really didn't.

'The music's amazing and, like, Elton John's one of those records that . . . I haven't met a group of people that after you've played everything all night and you put on an Elton John record that don't go, "Cool . . ." and kickback, and like it that the album's on. Whatever album it is,' he continued, gabbling about his hero just like any other fan, 'any of the first seven or eight albums, you put one of those on and everyone just relaxes. 'Cos they grew up with it and it makes you feel good 'cos of the vibrations in the styles of the songs, the styles of writing. And the way they take you so many different places on, like, one album . . .'

Axl related a story about how Elton John sent flowers to his dressing room after the band's first fateful show with the Stones. 'Yeah, it was great. He sent these flowers and a note. He didn't mean it against the Stones, it was meant towards the press and anybody else who was against Guns N' Roses. It said: "Don't let the bastards grind you down! I hate them all too . . . Sincerely, Elton John." That was just the greatest.'

Axl's third and last choice was perhaps the most surprising, however: 'I'm Not in Love': a No. 1 single, in both Britain and America, for 10CC in 1974. 'That song goes back and forth along with "Layla" by Derek and the Dominoes and Metallica's "Fade to Black" for me,' Axl did his best to explain. 'As weird a cross as it may seem, those three songs are my favourite songs of all time . . . But we were talking about when I was young. "Layla" I didn't get into till I was a bit older.

'10CC . . . I used to go to piano lessons, right? I'd go to piano lessons and go early, and I'd go to this drugstore that was very nice and conservative but had this liquor section that you weren't allowed into unless you were twenty-one. And they had magazines like *Playboy* and stuff like that. So I would go there early and I'd hang out for hours in this drugstore. Like, steal a look at these magazines. I was really into *Oui* magazine. The photography was amazing. And I'm just discovering girls and stuff like that and I'm, like, going with the girls in my school and stuff, in my class. But they're boring.

'But in these magazines, like, *these* are women and they're great, you know? All right. Well, "I'm Not in Love" was always on in this place. And the production is so amazing. It's this guy who is in love, but yeah, doesn't want to be in love, or whatever. Doesn't want to deal with it. He's contradicting himself all the way through the record. Plus, it's like, the coolest attitude. It's like,' he began to sing softly . That's so , like , nonchalant , so cool . But the production and the song has always stuck. Whenever I'm having a heavy emotional situation, or meeting someone, it's like I'll get in the car and I'll just turn on the ignition and that song will always be on the radio! I mean, that song messes with my life, man.' He positively glowed.

Just then the Cheap Trick *In Colour* album came wafting out of the hi-fi speakers and Axl's mood swung violently as he launched into an impassioned diatribe against Cheap Trick guitarist Rick Nielson.

Why? What was the story there?

'There was a thing in *Rolling Stone* where he said he fuckin' decked Slash. He didn't deck Slash. Do you think fuckin' anybody's gonna deck Slash with [Gunners co-manager] Doug Goldstein standing there between Slash and them?' he protested. 'It's not gonna happen . . .'

It seemed like the whole world and its big sister wanted to claim they'd beaten up one of Guns N' Roses. Why did Axl think he and the other members of the band provoked that kind of reaction?

'Because Guns N' Roses have this reputation,' he assumed a shrill, haughty voice, 'for being *bad* and the new *bad boys*.' He shook his head sardonically. 'And so, like, hey man, it perpetuates fuckin' Rick Nielson in the youth market and whatever else, and he's bad, you know?'

Another case of apologies first, ask questions later? It was my turn to be haughty.

'Yeah,' he nodded, stifling a laugh. 'But if he had any balls he'd apologise in the press, not in person. He can come up to me and say he's sorry all he wants but it doesn't mean shit till he says it in the press. Now Bowie's a different situation,' he pointed out, 'because Bowie hasn't talked to the press anyway. It's not like he went and talked to the press, OK? So Bowie can apologise to me and then when they see photos of me and him together they're, like, fucked. You know, "We tried to start a war and look at these guys, they're hangin' out! Goddamn!" And that's cool, you know? Like, Jagger was supposed to have told me off and then I'm on stage singing with him. That kind of fucked with them all.'

'And before that the papers over here were coming out with all kinds of stuff about the Stones and us. The *Herald Examiner* came out with a big piece, and it was great because then the *Herald Examiner* went out of business. It was like, yeah! YEAH!' he hollered. 'WAY TO GO!'

The actual story the old *Examiner* ran, according to Axl, 'went, like, *"Fear and loathing surround Guns N' Roses . . ."* and dah dah dah, and this big picture of me and AXL in these big letters and stuff. And then this whole thing about how some chick's scared I'm gonna come kill her cat.' He stared at me dumbfounded. 'Like, I'm gonna go kill a cat?' he asked, a pitiful expression belying the ice in his words. 'I could make a joke about it, but . . .'

Switching tack, I asked when Axl expected the new Guns N' Roses album would actually be out? It was the old, old question, of course. But I figured if anybody might know the answer to it, it was more than likely this guy.

'Hopefully, this summer the record will be out,' he said without batting an eyelash. 'But I don't have any idea about the schedule for touring. We definitely want a major world tour and we want to play in as many places as we can. So it's whatever the best timing is to pull that off the best way we can. I don't know if England will be first or America, but we're not trying to neglect anybody this time. It's just trying to make it work the best way for everybody.'

Asked which places Axl was most looking forward to getting out and playing, he was unhesitating in his reply.

'I really want to play all of Europe, actually. I'm really into England, but we've only played in three countries – Germany, Holland and England. Now I want to play *all* of Europe. I want to go down to Panama, too,' he added glibly. ''Cos you know they played Guns N' Roses songs down there to get Noriega out?' And it was true they had, the U.S. Marines flushing the good general out of his diplomatic hidey-hole with an illicit confection of AC/DC and Guns N' Roses tapes blasted out of speakers assembled on the hoods of their tanks for seventy-two hours straight before the previously impregnable Noriega nervous system finally collapsed and he gave himself up in tears to the heavy metal GIs. 'I wanted to fly down last night, and I should have done, 'cos if I'd known he was gonna turn himself in I would have been there. I wanted to go down there and stand in one of the tanks with all the troops,' said Axl, and this time I didn't know if he was kidding or not.

I commented that Axl seemed very happy and relaxed tonight. Had he had a good Christmas and New Year, perhaps?

He brayed like a donkey. 'I had the worst New Year's and Christmas in my fuckin' life, man, as far as I was concerned. I'm in a good mood tonight 'cos it's fuckin' over and I fuckin' lived through it,' he sighed. 'You know, like, I fuckin' hibernated, didn't see anybody. People say that's wrong. But it wasn't wrong, it worked out really good for me. Then last night I had, like, eight people here and I was, like, in shock . . . You know, I was into it but it's like eight people that were all close friends. Like, whoah! Immediately it was like, OK, we haven't seen each other and it's all heavy talk – this happened with my family, oh yeah, this happened with my girlfriend dah dah dah. It was just heavy. Heaviness all around.' He looked bemused. 'So tonight I'm just, like, ready to sit back and relax. I'm happy because today everything's under control. Tomorrow it's fuckin' over. *Something*'s gonna happen, you know?

'And there's only one thing left and that's this damn album, man,' he concluded enigmatically. 'That's it. And I mean, we may do another record but it's like, Guns N' Roses doesn't fully function, nothing ever really happens to its utmost potential, unless . . . it's a kamikaze run. Unless it's like, this is it, man! Like, fuck it, let's go down in fuckin' flames with this motherfucker . . . you know?' He picked up another cigarette. Torched it. 'And now that's how we are about the record. Everybody's like, we're just gonna *do* this son-of-a-bitch. And I just wanna shove it down . . . I mean, people are gonna say a lot of hostile things, in magazines and stuff. But I don't wanna spend my time doing interviews telling everybody that's into Guns N' Roses to relax, we're not saying anything against you guys . . .

'But, like, there's gonna be a lot of abuse aimed in my comments and in my words and stuff, and that's to the fuckin' people that don't like Guns N' Roses. It's like, hey, fuck you! You can like what you want but don't be saying shit about me. I don't go on in my interviews saying a whole bunch of shit about New Kids on the Block, you know?'

The hour, as the prophet sang, was getting late. Axl was still animated, though. The singer casting a slant-eyed glance into the year ahead for himself and his band . . .

'Let me say a couple more things. With the next record . . . the main part about this record is this is our *dream*. To get these songs out there to the public. Then once we get out there, then we'll fight for 'em with the business-side and stuff. But at this point that's not what's important. It's recording the songs.'

And, Axl was quick to stipulate, the idea of commercial failure held no fear for him. 'If the business comes down really hard on us in a weird way, then we'll make a choice: do we wanna deal with this or do we not wanna fuckin' deal with it, you know? The record will sell a certain amount of copies the moment it comes out, anyway. We could fuckin' live off that for the rest of our lives and record our records on small independent labels. It doesn't matter. I mean, that's not in the plans but it just doesn't matter, you know? And so it's gonna be kind of like, what do we wanna deal with? Do we wanna, like, be giving everything that we feel we have inside of ourselves to do the shows to our top potential and stuff?'

And, well, do they? Would they?

'Sure. But I mean, I don't choreograph things . . . I don't know when I'm gonna, like, slam down on my knees. There's a couple of moves I do that are always the same, 'cos it fits the songs. Like the beginning of "It's So Easy" or "Mr Brownstone". The rest is just . . . what happens, you know? And it's like, do I wanna give all that and fuckin' have someone spittin' in my face? Does it mean that much to me? No. I dig the songs, man, you know, but if you don't want 'em, fine. I don't *have* to give 'em to you . . . I guess it's how much you want the cash then, when it comes down to that. And touring. 'Cos that's what it comes down to, is making the money off the touring, you know? And do you wanna go through . . . Like, the fans are great, but the newspaper said you sucked, you know?'

Maybe sometimes the fans were wrong, I suggested?

Axl, predictably, did not agree. 'When the pictures are of the people into it, you didn't suck. Whatever they say. Somehow you did something that they liked.' He looked petulant.

He had often threatened it in the past, of course, but could Axl now really leave all this behind, I wondered? The band, his career in music? Not just financially, but artistically, spiritually, emotionally, even? If he wanted to could Axl really turn his back on Guns N' Roses and just walk away?

'If I wanted to badly enough,' he asserted. 'This is all right, in bits and pieces. But whether it'll take up all the chapters in the book of my life, I don't know. But I'll write in bits and pieces – whether I ever compose it into a book or not – for the rest of my life. I'll always do

135

that. But I would also like to record for a long time. And . . . I have to make this album. Then it doesn't matter. This album is the album I've always been waitin' on. Our second album is the album I've been waitin' on since before we got signed. I mean, we were planning out the second album before we started work on the first one, you know?

'This is the thing, OK? But as much as it means to me, yeah, if it bombed or whatever, if that would happen, yeah, I'm sure I'd be bummed business-wise and let down, or whatever. But at the same time, it doesn't matter. It's like, I got it out there, you know. So what? That's the artistic thing. And then I could walk away. It's like, I'd like to make the cash off the touring. I'd like to walk away knowing that, like, I can support my kids for whatever they want for the rest of their lives off my interest rates, you know? And still donate to charities,' he smirked.

'I'd like to have that security. I've never known any security in my whole life, you know? Some people are like, oh, why don't you give money to this or that? You know, you have all this money. I'm like, well, no, I got a certain interest rate and I bought my security. You bought your house, didn't you? I worked for my livelihood too, you know?'

But what did the money bring? What was its true worth to someone like W. Axl Rose?

'The financial aspect is to get that security,' he said steadily. 'I have that in the bank now and I'll keep it, you know? What I can spend off interest and shit like that, I'll do. But I don't wanna give away my security unless I'm like . . . When I was gonna quit the band, then I would have done that. Except I'm not gonna take Duff's money, I'm not gonna take Izzy's money, for something I decided to do . . .'

Last question. First question. The same question, in fact, that I had been asking for the last two years . . .

'It's taken a lot of time to put together the ideas for this album,' said Axl earnestly. 'And . . . in certain ways nobody's done what we've done. Come out with a record that captured, like, an essence of the Sex Pistols' spirit, and stuff like that. And then got taken all the way . . . And no one's followed it up,' he added pointedly. 'Well, we're not gonna put out a fuckin' record until we can, you know? That's all. So we've been trying to build it up. And now it's like, I'm writing the right words. And that's just really started happening in the last month. And now, as of last week, I'm on a roll with the right words for Slash's stuff. So it's taken that long time to find 'em. And, you know, I hope the people are into it. I think that the audience has grown enough. Has grown with us. It's been three years, they've gone through three years of shit too. So hopefully they'll relate to some new things.'

I asked Axl if he could be more specific about the new material. In what way particularly had it 'grown'?

'Well, say you go through something that like – one period of your life you become almost like a monk or something, right? And that's your attitude and you write about that. Then you realise that some of your audience can relate to that but they don't want a whole album of that. And you're realising that. And you have to go through different things in your life and then write about it. When you're writing off your life and not fantasy you have to, like, have gone through these different phases. And now I think there's enough different sides of Guns N' Roses that, like, *no one* will know what to think, let alone us. Like, what are they trying to say? I don't fuckin' know! There's all kinds of titles for the record, too. There's, like, *GN'R Sucks*. That's one of our favourites. There's *BUY-Product*, B-U-Y product, like, *Guns N' Roses – BUY Product*.

'So with all those different things . . . Because what I've been afraid of is just putting out one point of view, you know? And losing certain fans, losing people, and having people only see that one side of us. You know, we need to give a broader picture of Guns N' Roses. And I look at it like a trilogy – *Appetite, GN'R Lies* and this, OK? That those three albums were kind of like, Guns N' Roses can do whatever the fuck they want. It might not sell, but like, it will break our boundaries.

'The only boundary we're keeping is hard rock. We know that's a limitation, in a way. But we want to keep that because we don't want it to die, you know? And we're watching it dic. At least we were before Guns N' Roses formed. We were watching it just kind of being obliterated. By radio. By, like, all the stations not playing heavy metal any more, and all this crap. And so we decided, OK, we like a lot of guitars, we wanna keep it.' He paused, looked at his cigarette then grunted, 'That's enough.'

And it was. For now, anyway.

EPILOGUE

Losing the Illusion

Despite the vows of abstention and the endless assertions of righteousness and togetherness, the new decade began for Guns N' Roses much as the old one had ended: in the gossip columns and not, as they would have liked, in the recording studio.

On 22 January, Slash and Duff attended the American Music Awards: a staid music industry event held annually at LA's Shrine Auditorium, and televised live across America. Staggering up to the podium to accept the first of two awards they had been nominated for, bottles of white wine in their hands, Slash uttered the word 'shit'. The second time, when Slash began his speech, 'I want to thank fuckin'—oops!', the invited crowd, mostly aging tuxedoed industry barons and their mistresses, grew visibly agitated.

The obviously inebriated guitarist attempted to salvage the situation by going on to thank the Geffen Records A&R team 'for finding us' and the band's managers 'for fuckin' getting us there.' At which point the show's director cut to a hastily arranged commercial break.

ABC, who networked the show, logged literally hundreds of complaints from irate callers all over the country and the following morning the story made the front pages of both the *Los Angeles Times* and the *New York Times*.

Slash, however, remained stoically unrepentant. 'I sort of wanted us to be the fuck-ups there, because everybody else was so polite and stiff and unnatural,' he was quoted as saying in *Rolling Stone*. 'We were trying to have a good time, and I think out of all the people there, we were the only ones who weren't putting on a façade.'

The last time I spoke to Axl was over the phone, a couple of months after the American Music Awards, and just before *Kerrang's!* publication of the edited-down version of our interview in the last chapter. Looking back on some of the more inflammatory quotes contained in that piece shortly before it went to press—specifically, the desire to 'take out' Vince Neil of Motley Crue—I was concerned that some of his statements, made

139

in the heat of the moment, might be the cause of some regret later on and I wanted to check with Axl that he still stood by what he had said. 'Is this on tape?' he asked sharply. It is, I told him. 'OK, the Motley thing,' he began evenly. '. . . I feel childish now about my comments, at the same time I'm still glad I said what I said. But I do feel a bit childish about it and I feel that my anger fell into what I believe is Nikki Sixx's game of publicity. I fell into that but decided at that point that I didn't care. If I had to do it over again I might not necessarily make those comments but, at the same time, I'm willing to live with them.'

What if Vince Neil were to actually take him up on his offer, though, and come after him? 'Fine,' he said, unabashed. 'You know, whenever he wants it. I don't have the time to worry about going after Vince. If Vince wants to come out after me I'll clean up the floor with the motherfucker.

'I feel bad that we had to put the dirty laundry out in public,' Axl said. 'But I've never been a closed person. I've always been an open book and basically, you know, they took advantage of us in a lot of ways other than that particular fight, and we're getting tired of it. At the same time I wish the best for Motley Crue. Nikki Sixx is a survivor and I respect that.'

While I had Axl on the phone I took the opportunity to try and clear up another weird tale that had been scolding the phone lines out of LA— namely, that Steven Adler had been fired from the band. His continuing failure to kick his heroin habit was cited as the chief reason why recording of the new album had once again been iced.

'No,' Axl insisted. 'He is back in the band.' But he was definitely out of the band for a period, then? 'Yeah. He was definitely out of the band. He wasn't necessarily fired. We worked with [former Sea Hags drummer] Adam Maples, we worked with [former Pretenders drummer] Martin Chambers. Then Steven did the Guns N' Roses thing and got his shit together.

'And it worked. He did it. And Steven plays the songs better than any of 'em. He's just bad-assed and he's GN'R. And so, if he doesn't blow it, we're gonna try the album with him . . . and the tour,' he added after thinking it over for a moment. 'You know, we worked out a contract with him. He's going to do the album and, if he doesn't blow it, then he's going to do the tour. Then if he doesn't blow that he's fully reinstated.'

You mean you've given him a straight choice: give up the drugs or give up the band? I asked. 'Yeah, exactly. But like, you know, it's worked out. You know, it's finally back on and we're just hoping that it continues. It's only been a few days,' he explained. 'What's today? Saturday? It's only been since Tuesday that it's been back on. So since Tuesday it was on and he's doing great.'

How much of the new album had they actually got done before the situation with Steven forced them to pull out yet again? Another pause. 'Ah . . . we don't start recording til May First. We pulled out of the studio and went back and rewrote some of the songs, and . . . because of the Steven situation. But what was cool about the Steven situation is that it made the four of us realise that we'd got to get our shit together. Because if we bring in Martin Chambers then we better have the songs *down*. You know, so then we worked out eleven songs in a week, that we really had down. And so we worked those out and got those tight. And then worked on a bunch of things in rehearsal, you know, with other drummers, and got all of our weak areas pretty tight. "But here is new news,' he interrupted himself, brightening suddenly. 'There is a new member of GN'R.'

What? I was caught off-guard. There was a new member of Guns N' Roses? 'Yeah.' Who? 'Uh, a guy named Dizzy.' I repeated myself—who? 'Dizzy. D-I-Z-Z-Y.' Does he have a last name? I inquired. 'I don't know,' Axl replied, deliberately oblique. 'We just call him Dizzy. But he's the sixth member of Guns N' Roses. He's our keyboard player and piano player.' Would I know him from anywhere? I asked, still not sure if Axl was putting me on or not. 'He was in a band out here called The Wild. And he used to be our next door neighbour. He was actually asked to join three or four years ago. But the very same day that we decided we were gonna ask Dizzy to join the band he was in a car wreck and had his hand smashed, so he had to get pins and stuff put in it. Then he came into rehearsal a few months ago and played three songs that he'd never heard before, songs that we didn't even plan having piano in, that were heavy metal. But he put heavy metal piano into it, you know? And it was amazing.

'So the other day, Monday, I found out he was going to be put out on the streets . . . no, it was a Sunday night. So I called Alan on Monday and I said, secure this guy, hire him, write up the contracts. Put him on salary and give him an advance so he can get an apartment. So now we have a piano player . . .' And that was it. Apart from a last brief inquiry as to whether he had received some Charles Bukowski books he'd asked me to send him—'Yeah, I'm on my seventh one now, dude!' he barked—for a myriad of reasons both personal and, as ever, stubbornly unprofessional, the shutters came down after that. With the exception of a solitary brief interview with *Rolling Stone*'s Kim Neely, which he later went to great pains to disavow to an audience in New York—'If you want to read it, steal it!' he cried. Axl has since refused to speak in public—to me or anyone else.

True to form, the band never did make that May 1 date with Mike Clink in the recording studio. Instead, on 28 April, Axl married his longstanding girlfriend, Erin, at Cupid's Inn, Las Vegas—then filed for divorce less than forty eight hours later. The marriage was officially annulled six months later. On more familiar ground, Izzy was arrested for urinating in an ashtray on an aeroplane. And then, in May 1990, it was announced to the world that Steven Adler's problems with heroin had finally proved insurmountable and that, regrettably, he was now, officially, no longer a member of Guns N' Roses.

'All Steven lived for was sex, drugs and rock 'n' roll—in that order,' Slash told *Rolling Stone*. 'Maybe drugs, sex and rock 'n' roll. Then it was drugs and rock 'n' roll. Then it was just drugs.' He said he had tried to keep in touch with his former boyhood friend but that it had proved difficult. 'I did keep in touch. I'd pop into his house every now and then to see how he was doing. I stuck with him, as you'd do for a loved one. Then he started getting on my case, saying, "I've heard you guys are all on heroin and what's the difference, blah blah blah . . ." And finally I couldn't talk to him any more. I'd take him out to dinner and it would turn into this huge fight, to the point where I couldn't take it. So now I don't see him any more. I call his doctor and I think about him a lot. And I worry. 'Cos it's a scary thing. He was my best friend for a long time.'

It was Slash who first spotted Matt Sorum when he caught the drummer playing with The Cult at the Universal Amphitheatre, in LA, some weeks before and 'figured I'd just try to steal him,' as he told *Vox*. 'The main thing I noticed was that the drummer was great and I said, "Well, why can't we find a drummer like that? What's the problem?" I was tearing my hair out trying to find a guy who would fit in the band. It's not like we just hire some outside guy as long as he can play the parts right. And then I remembered that Cult gig . . .'

Work on the new Guns N' Roses album finally began for real in the summer of 1990. The basic tracks to thirty-six songs were reputed to have been recorded in less than thirty days. The first fruits of this sudden, unprecedented labour being a long meandering track called 'Civil War'— the most ironic flag-waver since Hendrix's wilfully misshapen 'Star-Spangled Banner' some twenty years before—which the band donated to the 'Nobody's Angel' compilation album, a fund-raiser organised under the aegis of George Harrison, with all proceeds going to the Romanian Angel Appeal—a charity set up to aid those children left orphaned by the Romanian uprising of December 1989. Then, in July 1990, a rough-hewn studio outtake version of 'Knockin' On Heaven's Door' found its way onto the soundtrack album to the latest Tom Cruise movie, *Days Of Thunder;* the resultant video—itself an outtake of a performance broadcast from the Ritz club in New York two years before—quickly shot to No.1 on the MTV charts, despite Axl's copious expletives having to be bleeped out

142

(something the advertising-revenue-conscious execs at MTV would never usually stoop to).

Meantime, having reluctantly turned down an offer from David Bowie to go to Australia and lay down some guitar solos on the new Tin Machine album, Slash became the only guitarist in history to earn the peculiar distinction of having played on album sessions by both Bob Dylan and Michael Jackson. Unfortunately, the Dylan recording date was a disaster; Bob only requiring him to 'strum like Django Rheinhardt' on one track, before inexplicably wiping his part from the finished track entirely. He did, however, play on three songs on the new Michael Jackson album, 'Dangerous'—including the first single from the album, 'Black Or White'—though Slash didn't actually get to meet the star in person. 'It's at once the most sterile and creative process I've been involved in,' Slash told *Select*. 'Everything is pieced together from samples; you use the same drum beat and chords, then later add things to make it different in some places. Which is so different from what we do. Michael hires out the studio for, like, ten years and shows up once a month. I'll probably never get to meet him. It's sort of weird . . .'

Slash was also invited to play on one track—'Always On The Run'— destined for the next Lenny Kravitz album ('Mama Said'). They had been to high school together, although, 'we didn't know each other then,' Slash said. 'I was in what you call Continuation School, which was for kids who smoked in class, that whole thing. But we recognised each other, jammed one night . . . he's a real cool character.' Slash also found himself being invited to play on some sessions for Iggy Pop's new album ('Iggy was in a mental hospital when I first met him. He's such a fragile, sweet, soulful, honest and sincere guy. I really love him a lot') and even laid down the lead on 'Hey Stoopid', the title track of the new Alice Cooper album ('a real sweetheart').

And then, in September, the band entered Studio One at A&M Studios in Hollywood and began laying down the final parts for the thirty-six songs they staunchly intended to use on the next Guns N' Roses album, which was going to be called 'Use Your Illusion', Axl was already enthusi- astically telling friends—named after a painting of the same name by modern American artist Mark Kostabi that Axl greatly admired. At first they bandied around the idea of simply releasing one massive quadruple box-set, but Geffen understandably balked at such an extravagant pro- posal. As an alternative the band suggested they release two double- albums simultaneously (with two different versions by Kostabi of the same painting) but Geffen were still sceptical. A compromise was proffered—to release one double-album, followed a year later halfway through what already promised to be a two-year world tour—by a more conventional single-album release, with the added prospect of at least one EP of cover versions slotted in somewhere else down the line. There was even loose talk of a series of EPs—one punk, one funk, one rap, one rock—and the probability of a GN'R live album at the end of the tour to kill off the bootleggers.

Whatever form they decided to eventually release the new material in, clearly the band was about to make up for two years of near catatonia with the kind of left-handed pedal-to-the-floor activity unseen since the heady cottage-industry days of the late sixties and early seventies. And perhaps not even then.

As indicated earlier, original titles the band began work on in earnest at A&M studios in the fall of 1990 included Duff's 'Why Do You Look At Me When You Hate Me'; a new, ballsier recording of 'Civil War'; Axl's beloved epic, 'November Rain'; an Elton John–style multiplot Axl shuffle called 'Estranged'; the earthy, blood-warming 'Breakdown'; the Stonesy raunch an' roll of 'Shotgun Blues'; plus another 10-minute monster about an Axl overdose, co-written with Slash, called 'Coma'; Izzy's 'You Ain't The First', 'Pretty Tied Up', 'Dust And Bones' and 'Double Talkin' Jive' (the latter pair both featuring lead vox from Izzy); and Slash and Izzy's 'Perfect Crime'. There was even an acoustic ballad, with Duff singing lead on, called 'So Fine'; plus a couple of Izzy and Axl Saturday-night specials like 'You Could Be Mine' and '14 Years'; and, of course, obligatory Slash and Axl late-nite flare-ups like 'Don't Damn Me', 'Garden Of Eden' and the Zeppelin-esque 'Locomotive; plus grandiose exhumations of earlier pre-Geffen anthems like 'Ain't Goin' Down' (not eventually included on Illusion I or II); 'Just Another Sunday' (also not yet used); 'Back Off Bitch'; and 'The Garden' (another 'joke song' in the tradition of 'One In A Million', though much more obviously played for laughs, co-written by Axl, Wes Arkeen and *RIP* writer, Del James—and featuring an unlikely duet between Axl and Alice Cooper).

There were also at least two new versions of 'Don't Cry', a maudlin ballad dating back to the very first demo-tape they ever played to Geffen, and an updating of a dry-eyed, tongue-in-ear Wes Arkeen tune called 'Yesterdays'. Slash introduced one track with some remarkably adept banjo playing, and Izzy played sitar on another. And although, as Slash put it, 'There's still a lot of songs about, you know, drugs and sex," there was, he was quick to add, a strangely romantic feel to much of the material conjured up on the new album. 'Which is something I believe in strongly, surprisingly enough,' he added wistfully.

144

By the fall of 1990, they recorded at least eight cover versions at this time: 'Down On The Farm' by the UK Subs; 'New Rose' by The Damned (the first ever punk single, with more lead vocals from Duff); 'Don't Care About You' by semilegendary LA punks, Fear; 'Attitude' by the Misfits; yet another version of Bob Dylan's 'Knockin' On Heaven's Door'; plus—going straight to source now and an echo from their down and dirty days in the clubs—'Jumpin' Jack Flash' by the Stones, and 'Black Leather', an obscure Sex Pistols numbers featuring a fraught cameo from former Pistols guitarist Steve Jones. And, most surprisingly of all, an emphatically metallic version of 'Live And Let Die'—Paul McCartney's hit theme tune to the 1974 James Bond movie of the same name was included. 'There's not a ton of really happy material on it, you know?' Slash admitted to *Vox.* 'Most of it's pretty fucking pissed off. It's very pissed off, and it's very heavy, and then there's also a subtlety to it as far as us really trying to play. There are a lot of semihumorous drugs tunes and a few songs about love going in whichever direction. Regardless of whether it sounds like the blues or not, basically that's what it is. It's like I think Jimi Hendrix said—'The more money you make, the more blues you sing.'' '

As always, Axl seemed to have more blues to sing about than most. In the middle of recording, on 30 October, he was arrested at his West Hollywood apartment, on a charge of 'assault with a deadly weapon'. The 'deadly weapon' was actually an empty wine bottle and the 'assault' was allegedly on his next door neighbour who called the police one night to complain that the singer was playing his music too loud. He was released on $5,000 bail, and the case was dismissed to the sound of loud snores less than six weeks later.

The last time I saw Slash or Duff was at the Rock In Rio II festival in Rio de Janeiro, in January 1991. The band were booked to headline two of the shows at the giant 170,000-capacity Maracana stadium—scene of so many famous Brazilian soccer triumphs from the past—in a ten-day event that brought together such diverse names as Prince, George Michael, Billy Idol, Megadeth, INXS, Faith No More, and New Kids On The Block.

With the new album—still then being touted as a double containing as many as eighteen of the thirty-six still unfinished tracks—already being mixed in LA and optimistically scheduled for release by Geffen in April, the band took the opportunity of playing in Rio to try out some of the new songs they'd been keeping to themselves for so long. That and a week of, to quote the local *O Provo* newspaper, 'sun, sea and sin' was hardly the roughest week on anybody's agenda. The band also looked on their trip to Rio as a chance to relax; to get out of the recording environment and enjoy a change of scene before the serious business of touring began in the spring.

It was in Rio that the band's management began demanding that all would-be interviewers sign a two-page document guaranteeing the band total control over all aspects of the interview and resulting story, including copyright ownership and approval rights—on pain of a $200,000 damages claim if violated. There was a similar contract for photographers, with similar clauses, including band ownership of all pictures.

The contracts, though almost impossible to enforce, naturally proved immensely unpopular with all sections of the media present in Rio. A host of important magazines refused to sign them, including *Playboy, Rolling Stone,* the *Los Angeles Times, Spin,* and *Penthouse*—though *Q* magazine, in Britain, exhibited no nerves at all in running a favourable cover story written by a close friend of one of the band's publicists. Slash would later admit, in an interview with New York DJ Don Kaye that the terms of the contracts were 'pretty harsh, but my feelings about it were that if these guys weren't gonna be blatantly honest and do what it said, then they were out to screw us in the first place.'

As Geffen Records publicity chief, Bryn Bridenthal, commented at the time: 'In 25 years of doing publicity I've never dealt with a press contract before, but when you deal with this band, you deal with a lot of firsts.' Nevertheless, the contracts were later revised—the $200,000 penalty was dropped—though still largely ignored.

The shows themselves, in Rio, were strangely disappointing affairs, distinguished only by some spot-on soloing from Slash, some trite mike-stand-bashing antics from Axl, and a band (now with Matt and Dizzy) playing together live for the first time, before 140,000 people, and doing their darndest to pretend everything was going according to plan. Bigger and better things would be expected come the full-on tour. But for now, as one wag commented, at this stage of the game it was probably a miracle they were even there all on the same stage at the same time.

The plan after Rio was for the band to return to LA where they would begin preparing in earnest for their first-ever headline tour of the US, scheduled to begin in May. Second on the bill would be Skid Row, themselves self-styled pretenders to the Gunners' Baad Boy crown. Before that, though, they still had the album to finish. Or rather, they now had *two* albums to finish, the decision having been taken to go the whole hog and actually release two separate Guns N' Roses albums simultaneously—to be titled 'Use Your Illusion I' and 'Use Your Illusion II'. In fact, with both albums containing over seventy-five minutes of music apiece, what Guns N' Roses was really proposing was that they release not just two albums simultaneously, but two *double* albums simultaneously.

Wiping the sweat from the palms of their hands, the head honchos at Geffen pumped up the press by talking in terms of 'history in the making', and privately reassured themselves talking in terms of 'a marketing first'. The band said they just wanted to wipe the slate clean. Duff, as always, had a practical slant on things. 'Two buddies could go out and instead of buying one double album, one kid can buy ". . . Volume I" and one kid can buy ". . . Volume II", and they can tape off each other's records. It's not to fuck with the kids, but to fuck with the industry and the critics.'

No members of the national, regional or music press were given advance access to the album, meaning that no reviews would appear upfront of the release date. Speaking in *RIP,* Alan Niven described the project as 'a cross between Led Zeppelin's "Physical Graffiti" and Pink Floyd's "The Wall". It's a record that's gonna amaze and frighten at the same time.'

It was virtually the last proclamation Niven was ever asked to make on the band's behalf. That is, other than to announce his 'retirement' from managing them, on the eve of their return to full-time touring, after Axl let it be known that he refused to finish work on the albums until Niven was replaced by Doug Goldstein, Niven's former junior partner in his Stravinsky Brothers management company. Many insiders perceived the split as an undisguised attempt on the part of Axl—the only one who seemed to have had a problem with his former manager—to take a more active role in the day-to-day management of the band, and hence much greater control. Neither Niven nor Goldstein would discuss the split publicly, but rumours suggested that Alan's silence cost the group in the region of $3 million. Word had it, the rest of the band only grudgingly went along with the whole thing to prevent a total breakdown of communication and yet another delayed release-date for the album.

When I ran into Alan Niven in Los Angeles later that summer I detected no real animosity towards his former charges; more a certain frustration at not being there now 'to reap the rewards of all the hard work we put into making the band happen.' And also a certain sadness over losing touch with Slash and Izzy. 'I actually really miss those two,' he shrugged. 'Beneath the tough exteriors they're both real sweethearts, and I do miss them.' But 'not the red-haired one though,' he added. When I asked him to elaborate, Alan puffed out his cheeks and threw me a baleful sideways glance that said you-know-what-I'm-talking-about. He talked elliptically of the singer's uncanny ability to 'hunch-up and turn every victory into a disaster. With the exception of that first tour of England in 1987, everything else we did—each little success we had along the way—

147

would always end up being a problem somehow. He made it very difficult to actually *enjoy* any situation.'

These days Alan Niven manages Great White—a major act in their own right ('It was amazing; Great White got their first platinum album the same week the Gunners got theirs) and relative newcomers Havana Black. He admits it makes for a quieter life after the daze of Guns N' Roses, but says he feels he'll live longer this way.

'Musically, a group like Great White burns just as bright as a group like Guns N' Roses, but it doesn't attract the same kind of moths, if you know what I mean.' He chuckled. 'I can't say I'm sorry I don't have to deal with that kind of day-to-day madness any more. It's exciting, but it's also a lot of pressure.'

Guns N' Roses' first American tour for three years—and their first ever as a gen-u-wine arena headliner—was scheduled to kick off before 80,000 people over two nights at the Alpine Valley Music Theatre, in East Troy, Wisconsin, on 24 and 25 May, 1991. As a warm-up, three 'secret' club dates were hastily arranged. In an attempt to keep them deliberately low-key, the shows were booked under assumed names and only announced on the day of the show. The first was at the small Warfield Theater in San Francisco, on 3 May. The band openly admitted they saw this and the other two club appearances that would follow, in New York and Los Angeles, more as live rehearsals than actual full-on no-kidding performances, and several new numbers were aired for the first time at the Warfield. 'Pretty Tied Up', the moody opener, was quickly followed by 'Bad Obsession', a morbid tale of heroin abuse much in the style of 'Mr. Brownstone', though apparently predating the latter by some eighteen months.

Another new number, 'Dust And Bones', went down well enough, but was marred by the tedious and lengthy jam that followed, with Axl off lurking in the wings while the rest of the band did their best to fill in the gaps as convincingly as they could. When the singer finally returned to the stage, decked out in cowboy hat and shades to signal the start of 'Civil War', the band finally hit some kind of stride, and 'It's So Easy', which followed—one of only five old numbers included in the set at the Warfield—had people up and dancing for the first time all night. Then it was back to the rehearsal . . . 'Dead Horse', 'Bad Obsession', then 'somethin' very Seventies', as Axl put it—a long, boring drum solo. By comparison, 'Out Ta Get Me' whizzed by, the perfect vehicle for Duff—decked out in ancient Ramones T-shirt, leather jacket, padlock-on-a-chain necklace, and cockeyed sneer—to strut his Sidney Vish stuff . . . Then Dizzy was tinkling the intro to 'Live And Let Die' and the spell was broken. A ramshackle 'Patience' followed and the crowd seemed as though they might be about to lose theirs. The band, seeming to sense this, had a quick on-stage confab, then proceeded to blast out another newie called 'Locomotive', which at least had the crowd rocking like cats on the balls of their feet.

'Estranged', Axl's rites-of-passage paean to pain, pussy and pissing in the wind, completed the 'rehearsal' and the band sent the house home happy to the instantly recognisable strains of 'Welcome To The Jungle' followed by the inevitable 'Sweet Child O' Mine'.

Eight days before the first date of the tour, they repeated the whole thing at The Ritz, in New York. Billed as 'An Evening With The Doors', the band turned in much the same set as they had in San Francisco and LA. Axl pointed to a bank of teleprompters mounted either side of the stage, scrolling up lyrics—even to the songs everybody else in the club could have sung backwards—and explained once again that this was more of a 'rehearsal' than a 'real' show. Starting with 'Pretty Tied Up' and 'Estranged', the band shuddered and rocked but somehow failed to make the sparks fly, the six members seemingly lost in their own worlds, thinking of bigger stages and unfinished album mixes, perhaps . . . leaving little energy for those much sought-after extras like 'chemistry' and 'vibe'. 'Right Next Door To Hell', written about Axl's litigious next-door neighbour, and receiving its first public airing at the Ritz, sounded as big and brutal as old New York itself. Nevertheless, it was the follow-up toon, 'Mr. Brownstone', that provided the evening with its first big lift of the night, hurtling down the time tunnel to the bang-on, pissed-off zeal of three years before.

'November Rain' also got an airing; vain, bombastic, self-obsessed, and probably far too long to really love, you had to admire the gall of trying to convincingly perform this sort of work to a crowd of rabid New York headbangers. They would neither have tried nor succeeded in getting away with it the last time they performed at the Ritz. But then this was a very different band from the one that had played in New York three years before. Izzy had been sworn off all drugs and alcohol for almost a year by the time the tour actually got under way. Duff had given it a sixty-day try round about the time of their trip to Rio—which is about how long it lasted—a couple of months. And Slash, too, claimed at the start of the tour that he hadn't used any hard drugs whatsoever since he successfully weaned himself off them a year before. Asked about his chances of wigging out again, though, the guitarist was philosophical: 'It's not something I'm worrying about. Even though I didn't go through any counselling, I think I understand where it all stemmed from and how it could happen again.

'I look back sometimes at things I've done, and I see that what gets me off is working real hard towards something, to reach a goal. We're not always gonna be the brash teenage hardcore band, because we won't always be brash and teenaged. Kids hate hearing that, 'cos it reminds them that they're gonna get older someday too. But I think we can go out and concentrate on the music; we'll be a lot tighter band on tour this time, and better musicians.'

He caught himself suddenly. 'But then when we go out there, we'll all go fuckin' crazy and those plans'll go right out the window . . .'

There were, of course, the usual bringdowns—notably the rain, which lashed down sporadically both nights; a security guard who was accidentally walloped across the back of the head by Axl's roving mikestand during the 'You gotta give the other fella hell . . .' section of 'Live And Let Die'; and a foul-smelling smokebomb that was hurled onto the stage during 'My Michelle'. Other than that, though, it was like they'd never been away. Returning to his home state of Indiana for a concert a few days later, Axl compared the fans in Noblesville to the prisoners at Auschwitz after discovering there had been a 10:30 P.M. county curfew imposed on the show. "I wanted to tell them they could break away, too," Axl explained to the *Los Angeles Times*.

Somehow, improbably, and without warning (save that the original choice of first single, 'Don't Cry', had inexplicably been nixed at the eleventh hour), 'You Could Be Mine' was released on June 21—in time for the worldwide release of the latest Arnold Schwarzeneggar blockbuster, *Terminator II* (the track plays over the closing credits)—thereby becoming the first new Guns N' Roses single for three years—accompanied by a Terminator-style video, replete with dead-on cameo appearance from square-jawed Arnie, whose onboard behind-the-eyeballs computer wisely decides that blowing Axl away would only constitute *wasted ammo*.

When the tour resumed after St. Louis in Dallas, Axl stopped the show after twenty-five minutes to deliver a lengthy diatribe on the perils of abusing the fragile relationship between band and audience. 'Stop! Stop! Stop!' he implored the crowd, while waving an empty whisky bottle over his head. 'Some selfish, stupid, idiotic motherfucker just threw this on stage! I want to make it real clear that if you threw stuff on stage, we will *leave*. This is not about us being badder than you or anything, it has to do with being responsible—both to the band and to yourselves. I got my philosophy on this,' Axl sombrely concluded, 'from Lemmy of Motorhead . . .'

And the band played on . . . At the Nassau Coliseum in Uniondale, New York, Axl kept the band and the audience waiting until almost midnight before he even arrived at the hall. 'I know it sucks,' he told the 18,000-

strong sellout crowd when he eventually took to the stage. 'And if you think it sucks, why don't you write a letter to Geffen Records and tell them to get the fuck out of my *ass!*' It was the beginning of a bitter tirade against a variety of music biz institutions, including the people at *Rolling Stone,* the editors of the *Village Voice* and John Pareles of the *New York Times,* all of whom Axl claimed had also, along with a number of Geffen Records execs, been 'fucking with my mind' . . .

One person who did his best to keep his head down throughout the constant storm that seemed to swirl ominously about the band, was Izzy Stradlin. The only time the rest of the band really spent with Izzy was on stage. He wouldn't even stay in the same hotels as the rest of the band.

It was all part of his attempt, Izzy explained, to try and remain as *normal* as possible in what no one in their right or wrong minds could possibly describe as a 'normal' environment. 'Right now, Slash is a lot better. But these guys, they still drink, they still party. Probably way too much for their own good. Fuck, these guys like to trash the fuck out of themselves,' he laughingly told *Vox.*

These days, when he wasn't actually travelling, which was most of the time, Izzy spent his time off stage either skateboarding, riding his bicycle, or putting in a little road work on the motorcycle he also hauled around on the road with him. 'I've been straight for a year and a half now. No booze, no weed, no nothing. I just stopped cold. I said, "Fuck, I should give this a shot." At first it was hard. When I finally stopped and then started going out, just riding around on my fuckin' bicycle, I thought "Wow, this is really cool. How did I forget all this simple shit?".'

In August, Guns N' Roses arrived back in England for their first show in the U.K. since the ill-fated appearance at Castle Donington three years before. The venue was the 72,000-capacity Wembley Stadium, in London and all the tickets had been sold within hours of going on sale several weeks before—not bad for a band whose only previous performances in the capital had been three nights at the Marquee club and one at the Hammersmith Odeon.

Arriving on stage predictably late (there was an hour and ten minutes interval between them and Skid Row—seventy more than officially advertised), Guns N' Roses exploded onto the vast Wembley stage like a nail-bomb at a wedding, Axl a tornado on two legs, sporting a red tartan kilt and shirt over a 'No Martyr' white T-shirt. Fears that in their contrary manner they would elect to play too many unfamiliar selections from the

still as yet unreleased 'Use Your Illusion' sets proved well-founded. Including the opener, 'Perfect Crime', the band performed no less than seven
numbers—'Bad Obsession', 'Dust And Bones', 'Double Talkin' Jive', 'November Rain', '14 Years' and 'Estranged'—which no one could possibly
have ever heard before, plus two, 'Civil War' and 'You Could Be Mine',
which had never been performed live in Britain before. Add to that, three
cover versions—'Live And Let Die', featuring a very wobbly vocal over
the intro and, to close the show in singularly offbeat style, a lugubrious
medley of Alice Cooper's 'Only Women Bleed' and Bob Dylan's 'Knockin' On Heaven's Door'—and it was inevitable the arrival of the more
MTV-recognisable 'Appetite For Destruction'-era material (of which, by
comparison to the overabundance of 'Use Your Illusion' set-pieces
there was only a handful) was greeted with a mixture of excitement and
relief . . . 'Mr. Brownstone', 'Welcome To The Jungle', 'Nightrain', 'Sweet
Child O' Mine', 'My Michelle', and the second, and last, encore, 'Paradise
City'—plainly, judging by the overwhelming reaction, these were the
songs the fans had come to hear.

Of the new numbers, only 'Bad Obsession', 'You Could Be Mine' and
'Estranged' really left a mark you could still recognise the next morning—
though making the otherwise compelling 'Estranged' the first encore was
perhaps asking too much of the by then bedraggled Wembley hordes.
'Double Talkin' Jive'—which Axl petulantly dedicated to *Sky* magazine,
to *Time Out,* and to something I respected years ago, but now I'd rather
wipe my fuckin' ass with . . . *Kerrang!*'—would have been amongst the
best numbers of the night if these things were judged by sheer power and
fury alone. But Slash's awkward, faltering guitar solo towards the end sent
the number into a tailspin and it never really recovered. And when Izzy
took the lead vocals on 'Dust And Bones' and '14 Years', which were
interesting, even mildly amusing for the first couple of minutes, somehow
the momentum that had been slowly building like a fire at the start of the
set was lost, evaporated into warm summer mist. The most tedious moment, however, was the unforgivably boring seventeen-minute drum and
guitar solo sequence, which had the Wembley faithful fidgeting uncomfortably and glancing impatiently at their watches.

'Paradise City' played the show out in style—hot white strobes flashing
like balls of lightning around the stage—and at the end the road crew
came on to lift the band high onto their shoulders. Slash actually exited
the stage walking on his hands. And then, just when we all really had given
it up as beyond a bad joke (what's beyond a bad joke? an *old* joke), on
17 September, 1991, Guns N' Roses released a new album. Or rather, *two*
new albums . . . 'Use Your Illusion I' and 'Use Your Illusion II'. Containing, in total, thirty tracks, with over seventy-five minutes of music on *each*

CD, mostly the albums are a rollercoaster ride through the runs n' poses of all their favourite heroes—only those heroes are dragged mewling and stamping into the '90s whether they dig it or not, doooooood . . . Aerosmith ('Right Next Door To Hell', 'Bad Obsession'), Led Zeppelin ('Locomotive', 'Coma'), the Rolling Stones ('14 Years', 'Shotgun Blues') and—yes, it's there on 'November Rain', 'Dead Horse', 'Estranged', and even 'Breakdown'—some young Elton John. However, with thirty tracks to chose from, it would be a miracle if every single one of them was a masterpiece, therefore it's tempting to speculate on just how much more dazzling and impressive 'Use Your Illusion' might have been had it been simply that: a single, trimmed down, entity.

Work as thoughtful and lovingly crafted as 'Coma' (from '. . . Volume I') or, say, 'Civil War' or 'Estranged' (from '. . . Volume II') proves that Axl and Slash may be one of the most inventive songwriting teams to work exclusively in the rock domain since Jimmy Page and Robert Plant went their separate ways over ten years ago. However, the quality of some of the other songs almost made me wonder why they bothered with them. 'Perfect Crime', for example, dishes up B-movie cops an' robbers crap with more use of the word 'fuck' than an Andrew Dice Clay story; 'Right Next Door To Hell' is great fun the first two or three times you hear it, but quickly palls with repeated listens. Then, there's the deeply self-conscious hobnailed-boot renderings of 'Live And Let Die' and 'Knockin' On Heaven's Door', or the dreary-to-the-point-of-real-tears 'Don't Cry'—which for some reason known only to God and Axl Rose, actually gets included (with altered lyrics) on both volumes I and II.

Much of the material is transformed simply by Slash's spellbinding guitar work, which is wildly inspired throughout. Indeed, the only reason I would want to listen more than once to trite halfway-house stuff like 'Bad Obsession' or the cripplingly banal 'Back Off Bitch' is because the guitar melody and the lead work is so breathtaking (just toss away the lyric sheet first). 'Garden Of Eden' is strictly B-side City in any sane universe, which of course, this isn't. And as for Axl's 'November Rain' saga . . . well, it's hard to know what to say except that it's one of those you either love or you don't. Personally, it sticks in my craw like a turkey bone going down the wrong way on a cold Christmas day, saved only by Slash's marvellously head-lolling guitar coda that at least sees the thing out with some sort of swagger—and at nine-minutes-plus it could use all the helpful swagger it can get, kidz.

'Double Talkin' Jive'—written and sung by Izzy—sounds like an old Johnny Rotten lyric sung by Iggy Pop to an ancient T. Rex riff, with guitar solos by Carlos Santana (that's Izzy, too). But what really makes it weird,

153

though, is that it works. Beautifully. Ditto the wordy and conceited and eminently danceable 'Don't Damn Me', and the jokey, honky-tonk, fire and brimstone of 'Bad Apples'.

However, with the exception of 'Coma' (this album's 'Rocket Queen'), 'Double Talkin' Jive', 'Dust N' Bones', and the pleasingly psychedelic 'The Garden', the really innovative stuff is kept for 'Use Your Illusion II'. While 'Use Your Illusion I' is a thoroughly enjoyable rock and roll album, its twin contains the real landmark material; a major progression for rock music in exactly the same way that 'Led Zeppelin IV' was for heavy metal, or 'Never Mind The Bollocks . . .' had been for punk and the Sex Pistols.

Material like the aforementioned 'Civil War', a contender for GN'R's very own 'Stairway To Heaven', and the spine-tingling 'Estranged', with its beautifully arched guitar melody perfectly matching Axl's bruised, aching vocals, was what Guns N' Roses would finally be remembered for. And the handful of superior rockers—'14 Years', 'Shotgun Blues', 'Pretty Tied Up' and 'Locomotive'—all proved that when it came to laying down the hammer Guns N' Roses could still dish it out as down and dirty as anybody would want it. Sometimes even more than they would want it, as in the case of the track 'Get In The Ring'. Originally titled 'Why Do You Look At Me When You Hate Me', and written by Duff as his sort of anti-establishment punk anthem, Axl had taken the basic structure and remoulded it in the studio into a shape that allowed him to vent his spleen against life, the rock press and the meaning of the universe in general, and against three certain rock writers in particular—Andy Secher from *Hit Parader,* Bob Guccione from *Spin,* and—yup—me. My crime? 'Rippin' off the fuckin' kids,' Axl calls it in 'Get In The Ring'. Writing it the way I see it, I call it. The same crime Axl always claims he is being punished for whenever the going gets tough and someone new takes umbrage to the lyrics of 'One In A Million' or the fact that swearing, brawling and drug-taking isn't just second nature to someone like Slash or Axl Rose, but *first.*

And in the middle of it all, the most incongruously moving, inescapably sultry tune Guns N' Roses has ever recorded: 'So Fine'. Written by Duff and sung by Duff and Axl, it is a moment of pure sex on an album that mostly revels in its own malevolent to-hell-in-black juices, and probably the best song Keith Richards never wrote.

As Slash says: 'This album spans our whole career. It's such a self-indulgent record, it might come out and everybody will go "What the fuck is this?" But we don't care, because it's ours. It's a killer album and it's not mainstream.'

Well, they've certainly done that. And yet, there lurks, as ever, a dangerous undercurrent that really does threaten to tear the group apart before they ever get to even *thinking* about another album together. Following the band's appearance at Wembley, in August, Izzy suddenly announced his decision to leave the band. You could tell things were serious by absolute silence that emanated from the Gunners' camp. This wasn't like when Axl did his 'I'm leaving forever!' trip; this was Izzy, ferchrissakes, and Izzy didn't usually fuck around when it came to things like this.

Certainly the rest of the band took the deeply disillusioned guitarist's decision seriously—going so far as to tentatively offer Izzy's spot to Jane's Addiction guitarist, David Navarro, before just as suddenly and as mysteriously as he had said he was going, Izzy did exactly what no one expected him to do and changed his mind.

As I write, Guns N' Roses are about to undertake the second leg of their tour of America where both 'Use Your Illusion I' and '... II' are currently nestled like a pair of Slash's snakes in the Top 5 of the *Billboard* album chart. What the future holds for them is anybody's guess. What's certain, at this point, is that this flight tonight ain't even begun yet and who really knows what lies in store for a band as hard to figure as Guns N' Roses? Duff says his next project is a solo album, with plans already laid to involve Lenny Kravitz in some capacity and a deal already struck with Geffen. Duff says he has hopes of enticing Prince into the studio to sing on a couple of tracks—though noting that Slash had recently referred to the Minneapolis miracle funkster in *Rolling Stone* as 'a faggot' that's probably unlikely now.

The last anybody heard, Steven Adler was putting a band together with San Franciscan singer Davy Vain. They're calling it Roadcrew . . .